T0061473

CONTENTS

THE MACAT LIBRARY

The Macat Library is a series of unique academic explorations of seminal works in the humanities and social sciences – books and papers that have had a significant and widely recognised impact on their disciplines. It has been created to serve as much more than just a summary of what lies between the covers of a great book. It illuminates and explores the influences on, ideas of, and impact of that book. Our goal is to offer a learning resource that encourages critical thinking and fosters a better, deeper understanding of important ideas.

Each publication is divided into three Sections: Influences, Ideas, and Impact. Each Section has four Modules. These explore every important facet of the work, and the responses to it.

This Section-Module structure makes a Macat Library book easy to use, but it has another important feature. Because each Macat book is written to the same format, it is possible (and encouraged!) to cross-reference multiple Macat books along the same lines of inquiry or research. This allows the reader to open up interesting interdisciplinary pathways.

To further aid your reading, lists of glossary terms and people mentioned are included at the end of this book (these are indicated by an asterisk [*] throughout) – as well as a list of works cited.

Macat has worked with the University of Cambridge to identify the elements of critical thinking and understand the ways in which six different skills combine to enable effective thinking.
Three allow us to fully understand a problem; three more give us the tools to solve it. Together, these six skills make up the **PACIER** model of critical thinking. They are:

ANALYSIS – understanding how an argument is built
EVALUATION – exploring the strengths and weaknesses of an argument
INTERPRETATION – understanding issues of meaning

CREATIVE THINKING – coming up with new ideas and fresh connections
PROBLEM-SOLVING – producing strong solutions
REASONING – creating strong arguments

To find out more, visit **WWW.MACAT.COM.**

MACAT

An Analysis of

Christopher Hill's

The World Turned Upside Down

Radical Ideas During the English Revolution

Harman Bhoghal
with
Liam Haydon

www.macat.com
info@macat.com

Cover illustration: Capucine Deslouis

Cataloguing in Publication Data
A catalogue record for this book is available from the British Library.
Library of Congress Cataloguing-in-Publication Data is available upon request.

ISBN 978-1-912302-61-1 (hardback)
ISBN 978-1-912128-44-0 (paperback)
ISBN 978-1-912281-49-7 (e-book)

Notice
The information in this book is designed to orientate readers of the work under analysis,
to elucidate and contextualise its key ideas and themes, and to aid in the development
of critical thinking skills. It is not meant to be used, nor should it be used, as a
substitute for original thinking or in place of original writing or research. References and
notes are provided for informational purposes and their presence does not constitute
endorsement of the information or opinions therein. This book is presented solely for
educational purposes. It is sold on the understanding that the publisher is not engaged
to provide any scholarly advice. The publisher has made every effort to ensure that
this book is accurate and up-to-date, but makes no warranties or representations with
regard to the completeness or reliability of the information it contains. The information
and the opinions provided herein are not guaranteed or warranted to produce particular
results and may not be suitable for students of every ability. The publisher shall not be
liable for any loss, damage or disruption arising from any errors or omissions, or from
the use of this book, including, but not limited to, special, incidental, consequential or
other damages caused, or alleged to have been caused, directly or indirectly, by the
information contained within.

CRITICAL THINKING AND
THE WORLD TURNED UPSIDE DOWN

Primary critical thinking skill: PROBLEM-SOLVING
Secondary critical thinking skill: EVALUATION

Few works of history have succeeded so completely in forcing their readers to take a fresh look at the evidence as Christopher Hill's *The World Turned Upside Down* – and that achievement is rooted firmly in Hill's exceptional problem-solving skills.

Traditional interpretations of the English Civil War concentrated heavily on a top-down analysis of the doings of king and parliament. Hill looked at 'history from below,' focusing instead on the ways in which the people of Britain saw the society they lived in and nurtured hopes for a better future. Failing to understand these factors – and the impact they had on the origins and outcomes of the wars of the 1640s – means failing to understand the historical period. In this sense, Hill's influential work is a great example of the problem-solving skills of asking productive questions and generating alternative possibilities. It forced a generation of historians to re-evaluate the things they thought they knew about a key pivot point in British history – and went on to influence the generations that came after them.

ABOUT THE AUTHOR OF THE ORIGINAL WORK

Christopher Hill was born in York, England, in 1912. Despite being brought up a Methodist, he became interested in communism as a student at Oxford. Hill opted for a career in academia—interrupted only by his participation in World War II—and held a number of posts, including that of master of Balliol College, Oxford. He died in 2003, and will best be remembered for his role in the Communist Party Historians Group, where he helped revolutionize the study of history by focusing on the role of ordinary people, rather than on kings and politicians.

ABOUT THE AUTHOR OF THE ANALYSIS

Dr Harman Bhogal holds a PhD in early modern history from Birkbeck, London.

Dr Liam Haydon holds a doctorate in English literature from Manchester University. He is currently a postdoctoral researcher at the University of Kent, where his work focuses on the cultural impacts of global trade in the early seventeenth century.

ABOUT MACAT

GREAT WORKS FOR CRITICAL THINKING

Macat is focused on making the ideas of the world's great thinkers accessible and comprehensible to everybody, everywhere, in ways that promote the development of enhanced critical thinking skills.

It works with leading academics from the world's top universities to produce new analyses that focus on the ideas and the impact of the most influential works ever written across a wide variety of academic disciplines. Each of the works that sit at the heart of its growing library is an enduring example of great thinking. But by setting them in context – and looking at the influences that shaped their authors, as well as the responses they provoked – Macat encourages readers to look at these classics and game-changers with fresh eyes. Readers learn to think, engage and challenge their ideas, rather than simply accepting them.

'Macat offers an amazing first-of-its-kind tool for
interdisciplinary learning and research. Its focus on works
that transformed their disciplines and its rigorous approach,
drawing on the world's leading experts and educational institutions,
opens up a world-class education to anyone.'

Andreas Schleicher,
Director for Education and Skills, Organisation for Economic
Co-operation and Development

'Macat is taking on some of the major challenges in university
education ... They have drawn together a strong team of active
academics who are producing teaching materials that are
novel in the breadth of their approach.'

Prof Lord Broers,
former Vice-Chancellor of the University of Cambridge

'The Macat vision is exceptionally exciting. It focuses
upon new modes of learning which analyse and explain seminal texts
which have profoundly influenced world thinking and so social and
economic development. It promotes the kind of critical thinking
which is essential for any society and economy.
This is the learning of the future.'

Rt Hon Charles Clarke, former UK Secretary of State for Education

'The Macat analyses provide immediate access to the critical
conversation surrounding the books that have shaped their
respective discipline, which will make them an invaluable resource
to all of those, students and teachers, working in the field.'

Professor William Tronzo, University of California at San Diego

WAYS IN TO THE TEXT

KEY POINTS

- Christopher Hill (1912–2003) was an English historian of the seventeenth century.

- *The World Turned Upside Down* demonstrated the importance of the radical* ideas generated during the English Civil Wars* of 1642 to 1649—a series of conflicts fought between supporters of King Charles I* and supporters of Parliament.

- Hill's model was an influential one; the book offers a broader challenge to its readers to think again about the society they live in.

Who Was Christopher Hill?

The historian Christopher Hill, author of *The World Turned Upside Down: Radical Ideas During the English Revolution* (1972), was born in the English city of York in 1912; his upbringing was deeply religious. However, as a student at Oxford, he gave up his Methodist* faith, and instead embraced communism,* the political theory founded on the writings of the economist and political philosopher Karl Marx,* according to which aspects of the economy such as industry should be held in common ownership. He later left the Communist Party, feeling that it was moving away from the principles of equality and revolution.

Following his time as a student, Hill immediately started out on an academic career. He was a fellow at All Souls College, Oxford, then a lecturer at the University College of South Wales. After fighting in World War II,* he returned to Oxford where he started the most productive part of his career. He helped to found the Communist Party Historians Group,* a group of Marxist* historians committed to a new way of writing history: instead of focusing on kings and battles, they examined the common people and their radical ideas and actions ("radical" political ideas and groups are those that call for social reform, generally through revolutionary change).

Known as "history from below," this would become the hallmark of Hill's career. He became famous for his work on radical politics in seventeenth-century England, particularly during the English Civil Wars between supporters of King Charles I's right to exercise power and those who believed that power should lie in the hands of Parliament. Although his own political leanings sometimes stood in the way of him getting on in his career, he was sufficiently well thought of to be elected as master of Balliol College, Oxford in 1965. He stayed there until his retirement in 1978.

Hill inspired a whole generation of historians studying what were originally called the English Civil Wars, but which came to be known as the English Revolution.* While some of that generation took on his aims and methods, and others strongly criticized his work, all were required to take a position on his ideas.

What Does *The World Turned Upside Down* Say?

In *The World Turned Upside Down*, Hill argued that we need to rescue the voices and ideas of the "lunatic fringe"[1]—by which he meant those out on the political extremes, the radicals who took part in the Civil Wars and the revolution that followed, in which a republican* state known as the Commonwealth was set up. Historians before Hill had dismissed the ideas of these people, thinking them distant from the final outcome of the revolution. Hill argued that they should be taken seriously, since they showed contemporary debates and contests that would otherwise be ignored.

Hill shows that the radical groups were actually a "revolt within the Revolution."[2] They threatened a totally different revolution—one which would get rid of property rights and capitalism* (the economic model dominant in the West, and increasingly throughout the developing world, in which industry is held in private hands) in favor of a more equal community; something that looked, in fact, a bit like communism. Even though this "revolt" did not succeed, success was a serious possibility at one point.

Hill argues that we need to understand the communities and intellectual currents that informed them if we are to be able to understand what the revolution was really like. He also shows that the social upheaval of the Civil Wars helped to spread these ideas; people were scared and excited by the new possibilities that the apparent reversal of the social order had thrown up, while the conditions of the wars encouraged and prompted people to move around. Preachers and soldiers, for example, could move around the country spreading radical ideas in a time before mass communication.

Finally, Hill argues that even though the radicals did not manage to completely overturn the social order, they did have some success. In the long term, the ruling classes had to take on board some of the radical ideas in order to establish their control—a real, tangible effect of the "lunatic" ideas.

The World Turned Upside Down offered a completely new take on the events of the 1640s and 1650s. It also showed how powerful the method of "history from below" could be. Hill managed to show that new ideas came from those at the bottom of society and not from those at the top, which made the lower classes powerful and influential.

The book itself was enormously influential; almost all historians since that time have had something to do with Hill's work, in one way or another. It has been through three editions since it was first published in 1972, is still on undergraduate reading lists, and is frequently mentioned and discussed in academic work to this day. While Hill's method, with its focus on conflict between social classes, is now a little out of fashion, his range of sources and his way of connecting the material he uses have meant that the book continues to be important. Many scholars have continued to build on and refine Hill's work, especially by adding material from the archives to the story he is telling.

Why Does *The World Turned Upside Down* Matter?

Hill's work still provides one of the liveliest and most vivid perspectives on the events of the English Revolution. The text is important for the breadth of its sources alone. It is not possible to study the period without engaging with Hill's ideas.

By focusing on ideas rather than actions, *The World Turned Upside Down* offers a possible counter-history—or alternative history—of the English Civil Wars and the short-lived republic that came after them. Although it is especially useful for anyone interested in the seventeenth century, students of any period can learn a lot from the text. Instead of trying to explain what actually happened, Hill thinks about what *might* have happened, and why it did not happen in the end.

By reversing the questions historians traditionally asked, Hill was able to look at the self-interest of those who eventually came out on top. He shows that the ideas of the ruling elite were not natural or inevitable, but came from challenge and debate, and from the fear of being defeated. By focusing on those who lost out during the revolution, Hill paints a much more interesting and revealing picture of the conflict in early modern* England.

Hill offers a way of working that is useful for any historian. He is willing to look at irrational beliefs, and see the social factors behind them. The social history that he developed in *The World Turned Upside*

Down shows us how ideas spread across groups, sometimes in unexpected and revealing ways. While not many historians today put their case as dogmatically as Hill, a new approach to an old problem can often help us see the world in a new way.

Hill shows us both the power of imagination and the importance of imagining new ways of putting society together; he challenges us to take a break from our own ideas of how the world should be organized, and to consider how it might be different—even if the world we picture is shocking to us.

NOTES

1   Christopher Hill, *The World Turned Upside Down: Radical Ideas during the English Revolution* (London: Temple Smith, 1972, reprinted London: Penguin, 1991), 16.

2   Hill, *World Turned Upside Down*, 14.

SECTION 1
INFLUENCES

MODULE 1
THE AUTHOR AND THE HISTORICAL CONTEXT

KEY POINTS

- Christopher Hill's *The World Turned Upside Down* is still a foundational text in English history of the early modern* period—the late fifteenth to the late eighteenth centuries.

- Hill's political philosophy and analytical approach—Marxism*—shaped the work's direction and content.

- Written during the Cold War,* a period when communism* was considered in the West to be a real threat, *The World Turned Upside Down* attempts to show how radicalism* and ideas that looked like an early form of Marxism are a real part of English history.

Why Read this Text?

Christopher Hill was one of the twentieth century's most important and influential historians, especially when it comes to the English Revolution* of 1642 to 1660—the subject of his book *The World Turned Upside Down: Radical Ideas During the English Revolution* (1972).

Having earlier published *The English Revolution* (1940) and *The Century of Revolution* (1961), Hill had already established a solid reputation as a leading scholar on this topic. *The World Turned Upside Down*, however, offered a fresh look at the part that politically radical ideas played in the English Revolution. Hill rejected the then-prevalent belief that social progress was a slow, gradual change, largely driven by people of high status and influence, arguing instead that the apparently lunatic ideas of marginalized people—those outside of society—give us a better understanding of the way society actually

> ❝ Political and constitutional conflicts, the expression and organization of religious belief, changes in the social structure and the growth of the economy, shifts in the general intellectual climate and the structure of popular belief—all were to be considered in their interrelations rather than in isolation. This basic realization unlocked some interesting potential for a totalizing history … More than any other individual, of course, Christopher Hill was responsible for instating this approach to seventeenth-century studies. ❞
>
> Barry Reay, "The World Turned Upside Down: A Retrospect"

works than a study of elite groups. Hill also showed how ideas, rather than actions, could shape society, and affect how major events turned out—such as the English Civil Wars* between supporters of Parliament and supporters of King Charles I,* and the republican* state (a state without a monarch) that followed it.

Over the last 40 years, other academic work has superseded some of the things discussed in *The World Turned Upside Down*. But it is still a valuable set of sources and insights into the English Revolution. Few books on the period, before or since, have dealt with such a wide range of sources and ideas, and many of the ideas and arguments in the book have become the foundation for further work, both by Hill and by others.

Author's Life

Christopher Hill was born in the English city of York in 1912. He was brought up in a deeply religious family that was strongly involved in the Methodist* Church in York (Methodism being a denomination of the Protestant* branch of the Christian faith). The Methodist circuit preacher T. S. Gregory (1897–1975) and his message that "we are all one in the eyes of the Lord" left a deep impression on Hill.[1] He was also impressed by the egalitarian* message of Christianity (the message that all should be equal), which taught that the great and mighty would be humbled while the poor and needy would be raised up. When he was still an undergraduate at Oxford, however, Hill turned away from the Christian faith, and embraced communism instead. Communism is an ideology that, even though it rejects Christianity, Hill found compatible with his belief in the fundamental freedom and equality of humans.

Hill was drawn toward communism in the 1930s. The economic crisis in the United States known as the Wall Street Crash* of 1929 led to a prolonged and severe economic downturn known as the Great Depression;* for people like Hill, this seemed to highlight what was wrong with the capitalist* economic system, whereby the welfare of working people was routinely sacrificed for the greedy pursuit of wealth. Communism, on the other hand, seemed to offer a real alternative to capitalism: it not only put forward an idea about running the economy that seemed to avoid the problems of capitalism, by holding industry in common ownership, for example, but also offered an egalitarian vision, according to which everybody worked side by side to achieve an ideal society.

The impact communism had on historians in British universities was particularly strong. In 1946, they came together to form the Communist Party Historians Group,* part of the Communist Party of Great Britain. Some members of this group, including Hill and some non-Marxist historians, launched the academic journal *Past and Present* in 1952.

After a long career as a historian and master of Balliol College, Oxford, Hill died in February 2003.

Author's Background
The main context for *The World Turned Upside Down* was the struggle

between communism and capitalism being played out in the Cold War. Although Hill left the Communist Party in 1957 after the Soviet Union* invaded Hungary in 1956 to brutally suppress protests against communist rule, he did not completely abandon the idea of communism. Hill's personal belief that a more perfect society had to be made here on earth explains his interest in the Puritan* radicals, a group of Protestants who argued that the Roman Catholic faith was still too influential, and who sought to purify their own Church. They preached that heaven could be found on earth in a perfect social and economic system.

Along with the other members of the Communist Party Historians Group, Hill wanted to prove there was a revolutionary tradition in British history by presenting "history from below"—an approach to historical research and analysis that highlighted how important the history of the common people was and how important social conditions were in shaping history. "History from below" also hoped to inspire activism in the here and now. The book was, in fact, part of a series on popular rebellions, edited by the Medieval scholar and former member of the Communist Party Historians Group, Rodney Hilton.*

Hill wanted to show that the ideas of the Puritan radicals were the ideas of the common man and that these ideas went against the agenda of the bourgeoisie*—in Marxist theory, the group of people who have access to capital and, therefore, are able to monopolize production. He argued that these ideas represent an element of class conflict in English history that had never been recognized before—a conflict that is at the heart of the Marxist interpretation of history. By concentrating on ordinary people and by trying to rehabilitate the "lunatic fringe,"[2] emphasizing how vital and significant radical ideas of the revolutionary period were, Hill's work contributed to the "history from below" approach.

But Hill does not just lay out the religious ideas of the radicals; he also tries to explain them in the context of what was going on in economic, political, and social terms. The originality and influential nature of the work lies in its status as a total history of the Puritan radicals.

NOTES

1 Penelope J. Corfield, "'We Are All One in the Eyes of the Lord': Christopher Hill and the Historical Meanings of Radical Religion," *History Workshop Journal* 58 (2004): 115.

2 Christopher Hill, *The World Turned Upside Down: Radical Ideas During the English Revolution* (London: Temple Smith, 1972, reprinted London: Penguin, 1991), 16.

MODULE 2
ACADEMIC CONTEXT

KEY POINTS

- Historians of the English Revolution* examine the causes, outcomes, and aftermath of the English Civil Wars*—a conflict fought to settle the question of whether power should lie in the hands of the king or Parliament.
- Most historians preferred to conduct research and interpretation based on the actions of elite groups and people.
- Hill argued that we need to see the revolution as a broad, society-wide change that allowed unique freedom of thought.

The Work In Its Context

What Christopher Hill set out to do in *The World Turned Upside Down* was challenge the traditional view of English history as resulting from evolutionary change: that is, the view that it had come about gradually and with very little upheaval or disruption. Hill wanted to underline how important class conflict had been in English history; the English Revolution affected every section of society, he thought, and had produced the potential to change society in a more dramatic way than people had previously considered.

Historians were becoming much more interested in social history, thanks in part to the efforts of Hill himself, and were interested in shedding light on obscure beliefs in alchemy, astrology, and natural magic, for example, that up until then had been ignored. The reason why they had been ignored was the interpretation of English history known as "Whiggish." According to this interpretation, history can be understood as a progressive evolution in the direction of an increasingly

> ❝ We may find that the obscure men and women who figure in this book, together with some not so obscure, speak to us more directly than Charles I or Pym or General Monck, who appear as history-makers in the text-books. This would in itself be a satisfactorily upside-down thought to come away with. ❞
>
> Christopher Hill, *The World Turned Upside Down: Radical Ideas During the English Revolution*

socially liberated and intellectually enlightened society. Many historians working at the same time as Hill wanted to concentrate on incidents and ideas that seemed to show how this evolution worked. They focused on things like scientific discoveries or political developments that led to a wider democracy, rather than on ideas that did not fit in with this concept of progress. This was perhaps because they seemed irrational—as in the case of alchemy, for instance. The Marxist* historian E. P. Thompson* described this attitude as "the enormous condescension of posterity" and tried to persuade historians not to buy into it.[1]

Overview of the Field

The year before *The World Turned Upside Down* appeared, Hill's student David Underdown* published his own book on the revolution, *Pride's Purge*. Underdown rejected Hill's Marxism, concentrating instead on the elite groups, especially royalists, who had contributed to the English Revolution. But despite his focus on the major events of the English Civil Wars, Underdown emphasized "the relationship between politics at the national and grassroots levels,"[2] even though his framework went against Hill's in many ways. Underdown's work showed that all types of historians were realizing they needed a broader understanding of the revolutionary period, and that this understanding would come from sources outside of the traditional elites.

At this time, there were some historians who focused on political issues and divisions at the top of society, and some who belonged, directly or indirectly, to the French *Annales* school,* a school of thought that concentrated on the importance of social history—the study of the experiences of "ordinary" people. Hill's approach of writing "history from below" similarly aimed to focus on the history of the common people; this was in contrast to the "great men" approach, which concentrated on political leaders and high politics. The *Annales* school had a different way of studying history, however; instead of dividing it up into different fields—economics, politics, sociology, religion, and so on—they looked at history as a whole, in order to work out how these fields came together to produce events, crises, or social change.

Academic Influences

Probably the most important influence on Hill's work was the British historian Keith Thomas's* book *Religion and the Decline of Magic*, which set out to seriously investigate supernatural beliefs in sixteenth- and seventeenth-century England. Thomas's work highlighted the fact that what looked like strange or ridiculous beliefs were actually worthy of serious study. Thomas highlighted the fact that such beliefs were widespread in early modern* England (England of the late fifteenth to the late eighteenth centuries), and were important in that they helped people make sense of the world they lived in, particularly as a way of explaining misfortune and suffering.[3] He argued that although such beliefs have "today … either disappeared or at least greatly decayed in prestige [this] does not mean that they are intrinsically less worthy of respect than some of those which we ourselves continue to hold."[4]

The World Turned Upside Down is very much a part of this trend. Hill says that he is presenting a study of the "lunatic fringe" that was around during the English Revolution, but states that "lunacy is in the eye of the beholder."[5] Hill argued that it is important for the historian to look at beliefs from history and to try to work out the rationale behind them, even if from our modern perspective they seem bizarre. He argued that this approach sheds valuable light on the society that created those ideas. Whether the ideas are true or not is irrelevant to the historian, who should be more interested in trying to fully understand the past. The views of the common man are just as important to this sort of understanding, and therefore just as useful to study, as those of "great men."

NOTES

1   E. P. Thompson, *The Making of the English Working Class* (London: Victor Gollancz, 1963), 12.

2   David Underdown, *Pride's Purge* (Oxford: Oxford University Press, 1971), 6.

3   Keith Thomas, *Religion and the Decline of Magic: Studies in Popular Beliefs in Sixteenth- and Seventeenth-Century England* (New York: Charles Scribner's Sons, 1971), 24.

4   Thomas, *Religion and the Decline of Magic*, 800.

5   Christopher Hill, *The World Turned Upside Down: Radical Ideas During the English Revolution* (London: Temple Smith, 1972, reprinted London: Penguin, 1991), 16.

MODULE 3
THE PROBLEM

KEY POINTS

- Hill was intervening in a broad debate about the causes and nature of the English Civil Wars,* traditionally understood to have been fought to settle the question of how much power should lie in the hands of the monarchy.

- Many historians, among them Samuel Rawson Gardiner,* saw the English Revolution* as an elite struggle for liberty against a tyrant king.

- *The World Turned Upside Down* demonstrated the influence of lower-class beliefs and ideas on the conflict and its ideological outcomes.

Core Question

Christopher Hill's *The World Turned Upside Down: Radical Ideas During the English Revolution* gives a comprehensive picture of radical* Puritan* ideas that sprang up during the English Revolution. The Puritans were a sect of the Protestant* branch of Christianity who wanted to eradicate the influence of the Roman Catholic Church on their faith. The main question that Hill set out to answer was: how much did these ideas and the way they were spread constitute a "revolt within the Revolution"?[1]

This question is important because it unveils a whole new dimension to the English Revolution. Traditional approaches toward the topic had always focused on the conflict between the king and Parliament, and between the aristocracy* (the nobility) and the bourgeoisie* (the section of society with access to capital to invest in business). Hill believed this traditional approach showed how history

> ❝ A distinct minority defied the church and suffered the consequences, for a generation or more. Puritanism, if not the Puritan Revolution, limped on, proud in spirit but with a heavy heart. ❞
>
> John Morrill, "The Puritan Revolution" in *The Cambridge Companion to Puritanism*

in general has always been written from the point of view of "a tiny fragment of the population."[2] This sort of approach hides the depth of social and political upheaval that was actually going on during the revolutionary period. It also ignores what common people were going through. Hill wanted to look at radical Puritan ideas, which he associated with common people and the landless population—the farmers, craftsmen and traveling tradesmen, as well as the poor who were traveling around looking for work. By doing this, he was hoping to bring a neglected aspect of the revolution to light.

But Hill was not just interested in radical activities; in fact he was more specifically interested in radical *ideas*. This interest in investigating ideas that had previously been dismissed as belonging to the "lunatic fringe"[3] can be seen as part of a wider trend in historical inquiry, in which apparently bizarre and irrational ideas were considered worthy of investigation and rescued from historical obscurity.

The Participants
Traditional studies of the English Revolution had concentrated mainly on the role of people of high status and obvious influence who played a major political role in the conflict. The English historian S. R. Gardiner (1829–1902) established the idea of a "Puritan revolution," by which he meant that the revolution was caused by Parliament struggling for political and religious freedom, with Puritanism serving as its driving force.[4] According to their Marxist* theoretical

positions—highlighting the historical importance of class conflict, for example—historians such as Hill, Lawrence Stone,* and G. E. Aylmer* saw the period as one of "bourgeois revolution," where the bourgeoisie (the moneyed middle class) managed to sweep away feudalism* (a society in which the nobility held all the power), replacing it with an era of free trade capitalism.*

In the 1950s, the idea of "history from below" was born. This new approach set out to highlight the history of the common people, instead of just focusing on the history of "great men." Hill's work was a conscious effort to produce a "history from below" of the English Revolution, which he argued was not about a single or simple conflict between the king and Parliament or the bourgeoisie and the aristocracy. He argued that in fact "There was ... another revolution which never happened, though from time to time it threatened."[5] This second revolution involved "the attempts of various groups of the common people to impose their own solutions to the problems of their time, in opposition to the wishes of their betters."[6] Hill's stated intention was to put the bourgeois revolution to one side and to look instead at the second "revolt within the Revolution."[7]

The Contemporary Debate

Religion and the Decline of Magic (1971) by the British historian Keith Thomas, which was published the year before Hill's book, is seen as the text that started to establish the focus on apparently odd or irrelevant beliefs as credible. Explaining why he chose to study belief in, for example, astrology, witchcraft, and divination, which are "now all rightly disdained by intelligent persons," Thomas argued that all these ideas were "taken seriously by equally intelligent persons in the past, and it is the historian's business to explain why this is so."[8] These beliefs cannot be dismissed as madness, but must be accepted as playing an important part in the world of the past. Hill's work follows this up, and he points directly at Thomas's work as an example of a historian "looking for rational significance in any ideas which the men of the seventeenth century took seriously."[9] He also widens the subject by focusing on the relationship between the ideas of the Puritan radicals of the English Revolution and the social, economic, and political circumstances of the time, making a connection between the ideas of the time and what was actually going on.

Other historians had helped to set out some of what was actually going on, which Hill uses as the backdrop to his study. The work of Joan Thirsk,* a historian of agriculture and fellow member of the *Past and Present* editorial board, was influential here. Hill speaks respectfully in *The World Turned Upside Down* about her studies of the effects of unemployed "casual labor" and "younger brothers" on society.[10]

NOTES

1   Christopher Hill, *The World Turned Upside Down: Radical Ideas During the English Revolution* (London: Temple Smith, 1972, reprinted London: Penguin, 1991), 14.

2   Hill, *World Turned Upside Down*, 16.

3   Hill, *World Turned Upside Down*, 16.

4   R. C. Richardson, *The Debate on the English Revolution* (Manchester: Manchester University Press, 1998), 95–6.

5   Hill, *World Turned Upside Down*, 15.

6   Hill, *World Turned Upside Down*, 13.

7   Hill, *World Turned Upside Down*, 14.

8   Keith Thomas, *Religion and the Decline of Magic: Studies in Popular Beliefs in Sixteenth- and Seventeenth-Century England* (New York: Charles Scribner's Sons, 1971), ix.

9   Hill, *World Turned Upside Down*, 17.

10 Hill, *World Turned Upside Down*, 130, 146.

MODULE 4
THE AUTHOR'S CONTRIBUTION

KEY POINTS

- Hill sets out to recover, and take seriously, the programs of the radical* groups that flourished in 1640s England.
- The idea of the "revolt within the Revolution" was a major contribution to studies of the English Revolution.*
- Hill's work examining individual radical groups built on the idea of "history from below," reflecting a contemporary trend for studies of the beliefs of working-class people.

Author's Aims

Christopher Hill's main aim in writing *The World Turned Upside Down: Radical Ideas During the English Revolution* is to recover the voices, thoughts, and ideologies of a set of radical groups that had previously been pushed to the side or ignored by historians of the English Revolution. He also sets out to show that by studying these groups we can understand English society as a whole much better. The revolutionary religious and social programs they proposed "gave form and shape to vague ideas that were in the air." This is why they can reveal some of the key influences on early modern* thought (that is, the mindsets of English people in the late fifteenth to the late eighteenth centuries), particularly among the lower classes.[1]

Hill also sets out to prove the existence of what he called the "revolt within the Revolution"[2]—"the attempts of various groups of the common people to impose their own solutions to the problems of their time, in opposition to the wishes of their betters."[3]

There were several of these groups and they stood for specific things. The Levellers,* for example, favored popular sovereignty*—

> ❝ *The World Turned Upside Down* is Hill's luxuriant celebration of all those religious crazies who populated English towns and some villages during the years of rebellion and revolution. ❞
>
> C. H. George, "C. H. a Profile."

the rule of the people. They called for political equality through extended suffrage (votes for all) at a time when only landowners could vote; they also demanded equality before the law, and religious tolerance. The Diggers* (or "True Levellers") called for economic equality—equal pay for all—by promoting agrarian communism,* according to which everybody would benefit equally from what was produced from the land. Then there were the Quakers,* a Christian movement who urged religious equality by calling for tolerance of other religions. They believed that God was in everyone and that the individual, subjective experience of God was far more important than any state Church's control of the religious experience. Finally there were the Ranters,* a religious movement who embraced antinomianism*—the concept that faith is enough and behavior does not matter—as the truest form of religion.

This picture of revolution is poles apart from the established way the English Civil Wars* are portrayed as a simple struggle to establish constitutionalism*—the authority of a constitutional government as against the divine right of a king to rule. In *The World Turned Upside Down*, Hill set out to prove that the English Revolution was about much more than the conflict between the king and Parliament. Rather, there were multiple ideological "revolutions" going on simultaneously, as demonstrated by the radical Protestant* Christians known as the Puritans.*

Approach

This desire to look into the history of the common people can be seen as part of a broader trend in historical investigation. From the nineteenth century onwards, since the development of political democracy, where more people were entitled to vote, and the rise of movements such as socialism* (a political philosophy advocating collective control of industry and communal land ownership) and feminism* (a political and cultural movement calling for equal political and social rights for women), interest in ordinary lives rather than the lives of kings had come to the fore.

Socialism and feminism are all about giving a voice to previously neglected and powerless sections of society, and this desire extended to the study of history. Hill's work can be seen as following on from works by historians such as Keith Thomas,* who set out to demonstrate the importance of ideas that until then had been seen as marginal or irrational, such as alchemy, astrology, and magic. What Thomas wanted to do was show them in their original contemporary context, so as to highlight their importance in early modern English thought. More directly related to the work of Hill were the English Marxist* historians A. L. Morton* and Frank McGregor,* a student of Hill's, who identified the Ranters as a group whose actions and ideologies deserved to be studied in greater depth.[4]

Instead of looking at the "bourgeois* revolution" (in which the moneyed middle class succeeded in sweeping away the medieval system of feudalism* by claiming a degree of social power from the nobility and ushering in an era of capitalism),* Hill wanted to concentrate on the previously neglected plight of the common man, as seen through the actions of the Puritan radicals. This was important in order to get across to the reader how wide and varied radical thought was amongst a section of society that, Hill felt, had been mostly ignored by historians. In Hill's view, the result was that an important aspect of contemporary political activism had been overlooked.

Contribution in Context

While the idea of radical Puritan activity being a "revolt within the Revolution" is Hill's own, it does draw on previous trends and studies. The emphasis on what ordinary people were doing makes this a work of "history from below"— an approach that began in the 1950s and set out to highlight the history of the common people instead of simply focusing on the history of "great men." A book that pioneered the approach of "history from below" was *The Making of the English Working Class* (1963) by the Marxist historian E. P. Thompson.*

While Thompson's work concentrates on documenting the social and economic conditions of the English working class from 1780 to 1832, *The World Turned Upside Down* is mostly concerned with the ideas of the common people as expressed by the radical Puritans, which Hill considers to be important. This emphasis on the importance of ideas comes up in earlier studies, such as Keith Thomas's *Religion and the Decline of Magic* (1971), which looks at early modern English belief in the supernatural. But *The World Turned Upside Down* was not just a survey of radical Puritan ideas. What Hill really wanted to prove was that these ideas had an important social effect, even if they failed in what they set out to achieve.

Hill was not the first historian to look at these radical groups. Morton, for instance, had produced a study of the Ranters in 1970. But Hill's approach to the topic was important and original because he looked at the ideas of the Puritan radicals as a whole, producing a vivid and all-encompassing picture of English Puritan radicalism in the 1640s and 1650s. The idea of a "revolt within the Revolution" ended up being useful to both academics and students by expanding the scope of the study of the English Revolution.

NOTES

1   Christopher Hill, *The World Turned Upside Down: Radical Ideas During the English Revolution* (London: Temple Smith, 1972, reprinted London: Penguin Books, 1991), 363.

2   Hill, *World Turned Upside Down*, 14.

3   Hill, *World Turned Upside Down*, 13.

4   See A. L. Morton, *The World of the Ranters: Religious Radicalism in the English Revolution* (London: Lawrence and Wishart, 1970) and J. F. McGregor, "The Ranters, 1649–1660" (B. Litt. thesis, Oxford University, 1968).

SECTION 2
IDEAS

MODULE 5
MAIN IDEAS

KEY POINTS

- *The World Turned Upside Down* analyzes the beliefs of the bottom half of the population.
- It argues that the surge in radicalism* during the 1640s and 1650s was in fact an attempt to remake society on more egalitarian lines.
- Hill's text was for an academic audience and, though approachable, relies on a good knowledge of the period.

Key Themes

Christopher Hill's *The World Turned Upside Down* argues that the explosion of popular radicalism of the 1640s and 1650s in print offers a unique insight into English society before, during, and after the English Civil Wars* and Restoration,* when King Charles II* was welcomed back to the throne and the monarchy was restored. Although the book deals with a wide range of groups, ideas, and beliefs, two key themes connect the material that Hill gathers together. They are, first, the study of what he calls the "lower fifty per cent" of the population, and, second, the notion that their ideas were rational, and neither mad nor unworthy of attention. Together, these two themes offer a unique insight into this society.[1]

Hill starts by arguing that because of the relaxation of censorship laws during the English Civil Wars "it may have been easier for eccentrics to get into print than ever before or since."[2] Historians are therefore able to have direct access to parts of society that would normally be entirely unrecorded, or else would be censored and filtered by the ruling classes of the day. Hill argues that by studying the

> ❝ It is no longer necessary to apologize too profusely for taking the common people of the past on their own terms and trying to understand them. ❞
>
> Christopher Hill, *The World Turned Upside Down: Radical Ideas During the English Revolution*

writings of these groups we can construct a history from "below the surface of Stuart society."[3] It is a record of the dissent, the unrest, and the desire for a fuller revolution with permanent consequences for the social order that was eventually crushed when the social elites were restored to their position of power.

Examining the radical tendencies of the common people leads to the second key theme of the book: rescuing the ideas of those who had previously been dismissed by historians as a "lunatic fringe" not worthy of study.[4] But Hill argues that the outpouring of radical ideas was actually a set of reasoned attempts to rethink the way in which society was set up, in an effort to defend "the poor against the rich, the common people against great men."[5]

For Hill, these ideas are important because they give us a glimpse of a "counter culture" that "would be different both from the traditional aristocratic* culture and from the bourgeois* culture of the Protestant ethic* that replaced it."[6] Instead of a society based on who your family is or how much money you have, these radical ideas offer a world organized around community, shared wealth, and individual freedom.

Exploring the Ideas

The World Turned Upside Down makes ideas themselves an important area of historical study. It focuses on the "English radicals who in one way or another called into question the institutions and ideology of that society," rather than groups that may have had more importance in the way history was traditionally told.[7] Hill provides, therefore, a range of particular ideas that came from specific groups: the group that "questioned the idea of hell," the group that argued for "the upside down world, where there is no property," and the group that proposed "sexual freedom."[8] These ideas are linked by their radical nature—the way they challenge and rethink aspects of society that up till then had been fixed and unchangeable. These ideas "would prepare men to accept … the idea of the material heaven on earth," so that radical religious and social ideas, rather than being irrational, would pave the way for a new, better society.[9]

Hill is arguing for what he calls a "revolt within the Revolution."[10] By this he means the "subsidiary episodes and ideas in the English Revolution,* the attempts of various groups of the common people to impose their own solutions to the problems of their time."[11] Hill believes that their activities were an expression of class conflict: the radicals, who were common people, could see how unequal society was and set out to change this by calling for an egalitarian society to be set up. But Hill finds that these groups were often "better at destruction than construction," and could not agree on how to reinvent the world once old religious and social structures had been torn down.[12]

This class conflict leads Hill to his third main idea: the fact that these radical groups were usually made up of the common people— farmers, craftsmen, and (especially) those moving around looking for work. The displacement of large parts of the population during the English Civil Wars, especially through the formation of the New Model Army,* a force set up to fight anywhere on behalf of Parliament, allowed ideas to spread quickly. It also allowed those ideas to be reformed and renewed. In fact, radicalism itself encouraged people to move around by making them understand the need for them to spread their individual view of religious and social questions: "It seems indeed to have been perfectly simple for any couple to team up together and wander round the country, preaching."[13]

Language and Expression

Because Hill is attempting to write a history that does not deal with "Charles I* or [John] Pym* or General [George] Monck,* political and military figures who appear as history makers in the text-books," he assumes that his reader already knows the basic history of the English Revolution and its key concepts, terminology, and people.[14] He also assumes that his reader will have heard of radical groups like the Levellers* (who called for popular voting and religious toleration) and the Diggers* (who sought to create egalitarian agricultural communities by cultivating common land during the English Civil Wars). Consequently, although he discusses their ideas, he rarely offers clear or simple definitions. It should perhaps be noted, however, that is it is often hard to define these groups and their beliefs and practices in a simple, effective way.

Regardless of the assumptions made by the author of the reader's historical knowledge, *The World Turned Upside Down* is written in a way that is fairly easy to understand. The language is generally simple, and the book is well structured into a series of short chapters and subsections focusing on a particular group or idea. Hill also provides short summary sections at the end of groups of chapters to show how they are linked to the overall arguments of the book. But students should be on their guard, as what looks like an easy style often obscures the fact that Hill is making broad links between groups or ideas, which are not as obvious or unquestionable as the book might suggest.

NOTES

1   Christopher Hill, *The World Turned Upside Down: Radical Ideas During the English Revolution* (London: Temple Smith, 1972, reprinted London: Penguin, 1991), 13.

2   Hill, *World Turned Upside Down*, 17.

3   Hill, *World Turned Upside Down*, 20.

4   Hill, *World Turned Upside Down*, 16.

5   Hill, *World Turned Upside Down*, 114.

6   Hill, *World Turned Upside Down*, 341.

7   Hill, *World Turned Upside Down*, 123.

8   Hill, *World Turned Upside Down*, 175, 270, 319.

9   Hill, *World Turned Upside Down*, 174.

10 Hill, *World Turned Upside Down*, 14.

11 Hill, *World Turned Upside Down*, 13.

12 Hill, *World Turned Upside Down*, 255.

13 Hill, *World Turned Upside Down*, 316.

14 Hill, *World Turned Upside Down*, 18.

MODULE 6
SECONDARY IDEAS

KEY POINTS

- The work's key secondary ideas examine the reasons why the radical* revolutionaries failed: the strength of the Protestant ethic* (the notion that Protestantism was used to encourage productive work and the accumulation of wealth and property), and their own ideological inflexibility.

- The power of the Protestant ethic shows the way in which powerful ideas could be deployed for both conservative and radical causes.

- Hill's work has had a wide impact and still influences new studies, such as the histories of women in the radical movements.

Other Ideas

In *The World Turned Upside Down*, Christopher Hill set out to examine the radical social and theological ideas of the lower classes (craftsmen, laborers, soldiers, and so on) during the English Revolution.* These ideas offered a program for fundamental social change and promised a more equal and free society.

Having understood the potential of these ideas, however, we then have to ask why the radicals failed to "turn the world upside down." For Hill, part of the answer is the triumph of the Protestant ethic, which he defines as "an emphasis on the religious duty of working hard in one's calling, of avoiding the sins of the flesh."[1] This ethic was used to justify a society based on the accumulation of wealth and individual success—concepts that the radical groups that Hill discusses often opposed. Hill argues that the radical ideas of the time were unsuccessful not for military or material reasons, but because they

> **❝** Abolish exploitation with the wage relationship, and labor in itself, to contribute to the beauty of the commonwealth, would become a pleasure. Coolly regarded, we must agree that this was never more than a dream: the counter-acting forces in society were too strong. **❞**
>
> Christopher Hill, *The World Turned Upside Down: Radical Ideas During the English Revolution*

were pitted against an even more powerful, entrenched set of ideas brought together in the Protestant ethic.

But the power of the Protestant ethic is only part of the reason why radicalism failed, Hill argues. *The World Turned Upside Down* also shows that, even though many of the groups agreed about large parts of their philosophy and agendas, they were somehow never able to join together in a single, united force for change. This was mainly down to quarrels within and among the radical groups—as Hill puts it, "their principles were too absolutely held to be anything but divisive."[2] Instead of working together to bring about social change about which they mostly agreed, the radical groups preferred to work separately for their own specific vision of religion and society. By doing that, they doomed themselves to failure.

Exploring the Ideas

The concept of the Protestant ethic is not original to Hill, having been developed by the influential German social theorist* Max Weber* (1864–1920). Where Hill's originality came into play was in applying it to the ideological problems and questions of the English Revolution.

The Protestant ethic encouraged the accumulation of personal material wealth. Making money, or worldly success, was seen as proof of personal morality (working hard, abstaining from things), and, indeed, indicated that you were someone destined for salvation—for Heaven. The ideas of the Puritan radicals, Hill argues, were entirely opposed to the Protestant ethic; he defines the radicals as "daring thinkers who in the seventeenth century refused to bow down and worship" the Protestant ethic.[3] The religious reformer Gerrard Winstanley,* the founder of the Diggers,* for example, believed that owning private property and denying it to those in need was in fact the greatest sin. It was this sort of thinking that fueled the radicals' demands for equality.

The radical Puritans did not stand a chance against the Protestant ethic, according to Hill, because "Protestant preachers in the late sixteenth and early seventeenth century undertook a cultural revolution, an exercise in indoctrination, in brainwashing, on a hitherto unprecedented scale."[4] The radicals simply could not compete with this; they gradually lost their influence throughout the 1650s, and all but disappeared from prominence (and the historical record) with the restoration* of Charles II* to the English throne in 1660.

The concerted effort to preach and impose the capitalist and individualistic ideas of the Protestant ethic was in clear contrast to the infighting and divisions among the radicals. For example, both the Diggers and Quakers* were opposed to the antinomianism* favored by the religious group known as the Ranters.* Antinomianism is the belief that mankind is saved by faith alone, which justifies the rejection of any kind of moral restriction on one's behavior. The Diggers and Quakers saw this as damaging to their cause and their reputation, and actively tried to distance themselves from the Ranters—even to "eliminate Ranters within their own ill-defined ranks."[5]

There were also divisions within the individual groups. For example, in 1656, when the Quaker James Nayler* came into Bristol on a donkey, imitating Jesus Christ, he was arrested on charges of blasphemy. George Fox,* the founder of the Quakers, denounced

41

Nayler and set about restoring the movement's credibility by imposing discipline amongst its members. However, this only led to series of splits within the Quaker movement, which severely weakened it. Ultimately, Hill argues that the movement as a whole changed, becoming more conservative and respectable. In this way it lost its revolutionary power, and became "a corner of the bourgeois culture whose occupants asked only to be left alone."[6]

Overlooked

The World Turned Upside Down is one of the key books on the English revolutionary period. It has been critiqued and reread so often that very little of it has been overlooked. Since Hill published his book, however, the idea of "history from below" has become much wider than Hill originally envisioned it. One key area of this has been a reappraisal of the contribution of women, particularly lower-class women, in history.

The role of women in the radical tradition was a little overlooked in *The World Turned Upside Down*, even if those who have expanded on the subject acknowledge the work Hill did, and credit him with encouraging them to explore the area in more depth. The historian of women in the early modern* period Phyllis Mack,* for example, writes, "As [a] historian who is also a student and admirer of Christopher Hill's work on the radical sects, my obvious first step was to examine the relation between radical prophecy and class hostility."[7] Mack used this approach to produce a book on the part that female prophets played in seventeenth-century England.

Soma Marik,* a historian who looks at the relationship between women and socialism, says that Hill was "the pioneer, who opened the doors of understanding to popular radicalism in its numerous forms. To recognize the role of women within the far left of the English Revolution of 1640–60, we still have to begin with Hill."[8]

The World Turned Upside Down continues to be useful, then, to those historians rethinking the place of women in the radical tradition in the light of recent scholarship in the areas of gender and equality.

NOTES

1   Christopher Hill, *The World Turned Upside Down: Radical Ideas During the English Revolution* (London: Temple Smith, 1972, reprinted London: Penguin, 1991), 324.

2   Hill, *World Turned Upside Down*, 373.

3   Hill, *World Turned Upside Down*, 16.

4   Hill, *World Turned Upside Down*, 325.

5   Hill, *World Turned Upside Down*, 252.

6   Hill, *World Turned Upside Down*, 371.

7   Phyllis Mack, "The Prophet and Her Audience: Gender and Knowledge in *The World Turned Upside Down*," in *Reviving the English Revolution: Reflections and Elaborations on the Work of Christopher Hill*, ed. Geoff Eley and William Hunt (London: Verso, 1988), 140.

8   Soma Marik, "Christopher Hill: Women Turning the World Upside Down," *Social Scientist* 32, no. 3/4 (2004): 67.

MODULE 7
ACHIEVEMENT

KEY POINTS

- Hill's work was successful in bringing marginalized radical* groups to the center of histories of the English Revolution.*

- Both the academic discipline of history and society more generally were ready for the kind of argument Hill was making.

- Some of Hill's assertions and assumptions have been questioned—not least, how broad the movements he describes actually were.

Assessing The Argument

Insofar as it achieved what it set out to, Christopher Hill's *The World Turned Upside Down* may be considered a resounding success. Hill manages to give a truly authentic voice to the various strands of early modern* radicalism, and shows that their ideas were not the ravings of madmen or social outcasts but came as part of a long intellectual tradition of social thought. Hill goes so far as to claim that "the radicals certainly had the best of the argument," at least for a short time.[1]

Hill also manages to demonstrate successfully that there was a "revolt within the Revolution"[2]—that is, that there were groups of radicals who used what was going on in the English Revolution to advance their own ideas, even if these were often the opposite of what those leading the revolt were trying to achieve. The way Hill handles the groups and their beliefs allows him to highlight how varied and complex the political thought and activity among ordinary people was. And by thoroughly examining the beliefs of each group, Hill comes to the conclusion that they all basically called for the same

> ❝ As we contemplate our landscape made hideous by neon signs, advertisements, pylons, wreckage of automobiles; our seas poisoned by atomic waste ... as we think of nuclear bombs which can 'waste and destroy' to an extent that Winstanley* never dreamed of—we can recognize that man's greed, competition between men and between states, are really in danger of upsetting the balance of nature, of poisoning and destroying the fabric of the globe. ❞
>
> Christopher Hill, *The World Turned Upside Down: Radical Ideas During the English Revolution*

things, to varying degrees: all of them wanted the "abolition of tithes [a sort of religious tax] and a state Church, reform of the law, of the educational system, hostility to class distinctions," and all of them called for social and economic equality.[3] Hill shows how the differences between the groups become "blurred" when they are examined more closely, even though the groups themselves usually insisted on how ideologically pure and how different from the others they were.

Achievement in Context

Hill's work was right for the spirit of his time in two ways. First, the study of history was ready for a change from the "great man" model, which focused on the thoughts and actions of those at the top of society and dealt mainly with "grand political narrative, intellectual contributions, and macro-economic issues."[4] Through the 1970s and into the 1980s, historians were increasingly keen to challenge those narratives, thanks to the influence of the schools of thought, such as the French *Annales* school* of historical inquiry, to which Hill belonged. Even though he was not solely responsible, Hill's influence and achievements helped to shift "scholarly emphasis to the study of shared mental practices or culture."[5] The emphasis on radical ideas in *The World Turned Upside Down*, even though those ideas were unsuccessful, helped to demonstrate the value of this kind of social study.

Second, *The World Turned Upside Down* was steeped in the revolutionary spirit of its own age. Talking about Hill's work, the historian of political thought and radical groups J. C. Davis* wrote that the text "was counter-cultural, and part of its fascination lay in the sense that, in the late 1960s and early 1970s, Western society was witnessing a profound rejection of institutional, social and moral norms and conventions in the name of individual liberation and authenticity."[6] When it came to the revolutionary spirit of the 1960s, it was the same story as that of Hill's radicals from the seventeenth century: for all the talk, to what extent did they actually manage to overturn the "social and moral" norms of the day? However, it is certainly no coincidence that Hill's book on the radicals of the seventeenth century came out just as the radicals of the twentieth century seemed to be on the rise.

Limitations

The work can be seen as locked in a particular culture and a particular place; while it sets out to produce a history of common people, these people have to be defined in relation to the time and place Hill is dealing with. For Hill, the "common people" are that section of the population who were not in political power and did not possess much material wealth. They include farmers, craftsmen, and travelling tradesmen, as well as the itinerant poor, including vagabonds, beggars, the poor of London, and the squatters and cottagers who lived on wastelands, forests, and common lands. But these social types are not static—you cannot apply them to every society throughout history— and this means it is difficult to determine the universal quality that defines these specific people as "ordinary." We cannot categorize people according to their occupation, for instance: a seventeenth-century Indian farmer or a modern-day American farmer will probably not have the same concerns as a seventeenth-century English farmer. Even the idea of wealth is an issue, as a craftsman is probably relatively wealthy when compared to a beggar. For Hill, the general definition of a common person seems to be that they are neither aristocracy* (nobility) nor bourgeoisie* (middle class and wealthy). Hill's concept of the common people, then, is something he has created to talk about the particular social, political, and economic circumstances of England in the 1640s and 1650s. The "ordinary" people of Hill's *The World Turned Upside Down* are not universal.

While the book deals with a very particular time and place, it does have ideas that you can apply more universally. The text concentrates on the importance of ideas, and on investigating how ideas come about. As a Marxist* historian, Hill was particularly concerned with showing how important the social and economic circumstances of the common people were in the forming of Puritan* radical ideas. The notion that material factors such as where and how you live can contribute to the development of ideas offers us many avenues of inquiry.

NOTES

1 Christopher Hill, *The World Turned Upside Down: Radical Ideas During the English Revolution* (London: Temple Smith, 1972, reprinted London: Penguin, 1991), 272.

2 Hill, *World Turned Upside Down*, 14.

3 Hill, *World Turned Upside Down*, 72.

4 Carl R. Trueman, *Histories and Fallacies: Problems Faced in the Writing of History* (Wheaton, IL: Crossway, 2010), 89.

5 Amy J. Elias, *Sublime Desire: History and Post-1960s Fiction* (Baltimore, MD: Johns Hopkins University Press, 2001), 31.

6 J. C. Davis, *Fear, Myth and History: The Ranters and the Historians* (Cambridge: Cambridge University Press, 1986), 7

MODULE 8
PLACE IN THE AUTHOR'S WORK

KEY POINTS

- Christopher Hill was concerned throughout his career with the social upheaval and revolutionary ideas of the early modern* period—a period covering the late fifteenth to the late eighteenth centuries.

- *The World Turned Upside Down* is one of a number of books that secured Hill's status as one of the foremost historians of his era.

- Though Hill has been challenged, *The World Turned Upside Down* remains a core text for the study of radicalism.*

Positioning

The World Turned Upside Down: Radical Ideas During the English Revolution most clearly reflects the two main interests that Christopher Hill explored throughout his career: early modern printed texts and Marxism.* By the time Hill published *The World Turned Upside Down* in 1972, he was already an established historian; the fact that he was elected as master of Balliol College, Oxford in 1965 proves that much.

Hill was becoming more and more interested not just in focusing on economic or social conditions, but in stressing the power of ideas. For him, the power of ideas was both a topic of study and a way of trying to understand history: "Historians are interested in ideas not only because they influence societies, but because they reveal the societies which give rise to them," he said in *The World Turned Upside Down*.[1]

There is a real contrast between this approach and that of Hill's early work, which was more obviously affected by his Marxist politics and his desire to overturn the idea that the English Revolution* was

> ❝ The breathtaking quality of *The World Turned Upside Down* rested not only on the habitual mastery of Hill's scholarship, the quality of his insights, the verve and moving compassion of his writing but, above all, on the architectonic brilliance of the overall design of the work. ❞
>
> J. C. Davis, *Fear, Myth and History: The Ranters and the Historians*

essentially Puritan*—the standard interpretation at the time. Hill wanted to push a Marxist interpretation of events instead, and had been moving in this direction for a while. In his 1965 work *The Intellectual Origins of the English Revolution*, for instance, he linked a variety of key thinkers in the early part of the seventeenth century simply because he saw them all as opponents of the idea of monarchy. Though this was criticized by some historians as over-dogmatic, it set the scene for *The World Turned Upside Down* as a history of ideas.

Integration

While Hill's thought evolved over the course of his career, there is certainly a thread that runs throughout. The most important aspect of Hill's work is that he wanted to reevaluate traditional interpretations of the English Revolution. Hill's works have been extremely influential in this regard. Most importantly, Hill was a key player in painting a picture of the seventeenth century as an "age of revolution," characterized by social, political, economic, and religious upheaval and turmoil. This interpretation managed to challenge and eventually overthrow the idea that change in this period had been more of a gentle and natural evolution, reflecting a respectable English desire for a constitutional government and social change. Hill wanted to draw attention to how important disruptive elements within the period had been, so that he could paint a more comprehensive picture of what was happening and expand historical understanding of the period as a whole.

This idea had been present in earlier works such as his textbook *The Century of Revolution* (1961), which proposes the idea that the English Revolution consisted of two revolutions: the overthrow of the monarchy that historical study has focused on, and the social revolution between the landed classes and the mass of ordinary people—an aspect that has, relatively speaking, been ignored by academics.

Significance

The World Turned Upside Down is now thought of as one of Hill's major works, and, indeed, one of the major works on the period it discusses. Even though the text brought together many of the themes of Hill's career, it did so in a challenging but accessible way, presenting the ideas in a much more sophisticated fashion than they had been presented previously. For example, his first book, *The English Revolution* (1940), offers a fairly straightforward view of the revolution as a struggle between the aristocracy* and the bourgeoisie,* in which the moneyed middle classes succeeded in sweeping away medieval feudalism*— under which the nobility had enjoyed the exclusive exercise of power—in favor of capitalism.*

This way of looking at the English Revolution emphasizes the importance of economic circumstances and the class conflict that those circumstances brought about as the trigger for historical change. But it ignores the presence and role of other social classes in the conflict, both in their contribution to the revolution and in the impact of the revolution on those social classes. In contrast, *The World Turned Upside Down* shows the richness and variety of thought and ambitions going on further down the social ladder during the revolution.

Even though the purely Marxist approach that Hill adopted in this text (and in most of his other works) has fallen out of fashion among historians, his interest in "history from below"—research into the lives and historical roles of "ordinary" people—means that *The World Turned Upside Down* is still an important text today. While no longer the complete analytical authority it once was held to be, the sheer volume of sources that Hill brings together, and the range of thinkers he covers, means that it is still an important part of the religious and social history of the period.

NOTES

1   Christopher Hill, *The World Turned Upside Down: Radical Ideas During the English Revolution* (London: Temple Smith, 1972, reprinted London: Penguin, 1991), 17.

SECTION 3
IMPACT

MODULE 9
THE FIRST RESPONSES

KEY POINTS

- The work was criticized for being selective in its use of sources and overly descriptive.
- Hill responded that all historians were, by nature, selective, and his work should be thought of as a starting point.
- Although academic fashions have shifted away from Marxist* analysis, Hill's work is acknowledged as one of the defining texts of its genre.

Criticism

The first major criticism of Christopher Hill's *The World Turned Upside Down: Radical Ideas During the English Revolution* focused on the method he used to conduct his research and his analysis. Critics such as the historian J. H. Hexter,* for example, accused Hill of picking and choosing his sources in order to support his arguments, without taking their original context into account.

Indeed, Hexter was perhaps Hill's harshest critic at the time; in an article printed in the *Times Literary Supplement*, "The Burden of Proof," Hexter mercilessly attacked Hill's methodology. The article, supposed to be a review of Hill's book *Change and Continuity in Seventeenth-Century England* (1975), was an unforgiving attack on Hill's overall contribution to the study of seventeenth-century history, in which Hexter accuses Hill of selecting his evidence to fit in with his ideas, of failing to deal with any evidence that contradicted those ideas, and of ignoring the limitations of his own argument.[1] The ferocity of the attack can be explained in part by the fact that Hexter was generally

> ❝ In several senses, then, a confrontation between these two men is as natural as that between the meanest dog on the block and the most lordly house cat. Hexter is skeptical about great themes in history. Hill is a Marxist. Hexter is an opponent of the idea that economic determinism is a key to understanding early modern England. Hill is its most conspicuous advocate. Hexter's output is relatively modest; Hill's enormous. Hexter's history is stylish. Hill's is workmanlike. ❞
>
> William G. Palmer, "The Burden of Proof: J. H. Hexter and Christopher Hill"

hostile to the Marxist interpretation of history, which he thought reduced history to simple questions of class and economics, with no other factors being seen as important.

The World Turned Upside Down was also criticized for being more about the story and less about the analysis. The influential historian Keith Thomas,* for instance, questioned Hill's account of where these radical* ideas came from. He points out the apparent contradiction between Hill's arguments that radicalism was an expression of how vagabonds, squatters (people who lived on land to which they had no legal claim), and itinerant craftsmen behaved, and that it was inspired by the attitudes of their social "betters": the leisured class.

The second main criticism was that Hill had oversimplified. Historians such as Bernard Capp* and Austin Woolrych* were concerned that Hill seemed to treat the radicals as a unified and coherent movement of social protest. Although Hill understood the divisions between them to have contributed to their defeat, much of his book does emphasize the similarities in radical thought rather than the differences. Capp warned particularly that you should not impose rigid categories—"radical" or "royalist," for example—on ideas and groups that were, in fact, more fluid.[2] There were also questions about Hill's tendency to think of the radical and the popular as the same thing, especially as Hill admits that the Puritan* radicals were in the minority, and could not, therefore, necessarily be described as a "popular" movement in that sense.

Responses

Hill responded to J. H. Hexter's accusation that he had been a "source miner" and a Marxist "lumper" (that is, someone who uses sources selectively to fit into his argument). Hill argued that all historians were source miners and lumpers to some extent, and that it was the historian's job to impose some sense of order and interpretation on the past.[3] Hill also continued to argue that "the Marxist conception of a bourgeois* revolution [is] the most helpful model for understanding the English Revolution."*[4]

Hill continued to defend his approach in later years. He argued that the whole point of writing history was to come up with something new, and so you had to collect and present the evidence that supported your particular argument. He argued that, while you should not ignore other evidence, it is natural when writing history that a historian will concentrate and emphasize certain aspects of a topic—Hill's own concentration on the social, political, and economic aspects of Puritanism instead of on its religious features, for example.[5]

Hill was not worried by the criticism that his work was more narrative than analytical—that it told the story more than it analyzed it. He later said that his main intention was to open the door for other historians to go further with the investigation into radical Puritanism in this period.[6] Indeed, in *The World Turned Upside Down*, he says quite clearly, "We need not bother too much about being able to trace a continuous pedigree for these ideas. They are the ideas of the underground, surviving, if at all, verbally: they leave little trace."[7] But he also says that more work "could probably discover more connections, or possible connections" between revolutionary and later radical ideas—proof that he wanted other historians to answer this call.

Conflict and Consensus

While Hill was aware of the criticisms aimed at *The World Turned Upside Down*, he defended his approach, considering it important that the topic of radical Puritanism during the revolution should be identified as a subject warranting more study. He also defended his idea that there was in fact a "revolt within the Revolution."[8] Other historians applauded Hill's approach because it highlighted the variety of political aims and activity going on at this time. But the question of how to analyze this activity remained—as did the question of whether we should buy into Hill's lumping together of radical activity.

It would obviously be impossible to get radically opposed schools of thought to agree with each other, and critics like Hexter were never likely to be convinced by the way *The World Turned Upside Down* was put together or the conclusions it came to. In fact, as Marxist analytical approaches to history became less mainstream (partly due to the decline of Marxism as an ideology following the end of the Cold War),* debates around the economic and class-conscious nature of the book died down; it became an important touchstone in the development of the history of the English Revolution rather than a cutting-edge innovation. Similarly, although critics will still worry about Hill's selection of sources, it is mainly thought that Hill's "source mining" gave the book a breadth and depth of material which has contributed to its longevity and continuing value—particularly when combined with other studies of the topic.

NOTES

1   J. H. Hexter, "Christopher Hill: The Burden of Proof," *Times Literary Supplement*, October 24, 1975: 1252.

2   Austin Woolrych, review of *The World Turned Upside Down* by Christopher Hill, *History* 58 (1973): 290; and Bernard Capp, "The Fifth Monarchists and Popular Millenarianism," in *Radical Religion in the English Revolution*, ed. J. F. McGregor and Barry Reay (Oxford: Oxford University Press, 1984), 184.

3   Christopher Hill, "Reply to Hexter," *Times Literary Supplement*, November 7, 1975: 1333.

4   Christopher Hill, *Change and Continuity in Seventeenth-Century England* (Cambridge, MA: Harvard University Press, 1975), 279.

5   Christopher Hill, "Talking with Christopher Hill: Part I," in *Reviving the English Revolution*, ed. Geoff Eley and William Hunt (London: Verso, 1988), 102–3.

6   Hill, "Talking with Christopher Hill," 102.

7   Christopher Hill, *The World Turned Upside Down: Radical Ideas During the English Revolution* (London: Temple Smith, 1972, reprinted London: Penguin, 1991), 381, 383.

8   Hill, *World Turned Upside Down*, 14.

MODULE 10
THE EVOLVING DEBATE

KEY POINTS

- Hill's work demonstrated the importance of radical* Puritanism* in the English Revolution.*

- *The World Turned Upside Down* emerged from the Marxist* school, and was a focus of anti-Marxist revisionist* historians (historians who challenge orthodox interpretations of historical events).

- Hill's insights have prompted many further interventions, which develop and add nuance to his arguments.

Uses And Problems

In *The World Turned Upside Down: Radical Ideas During the English Revolution*, Christopher Hill attempts to rehabilitate radical Puritan ideas that up until then had been dismissed as belonging to the "lunatic fringe".[1] This attempt was influential on later studies of radical Puritanism. In his book *The Quakers and the English Revolution* (1985), the historian Barry Reay* set out to show that at the time the Quakers,* an unorthodox Christian movement, were seen as a real threat to existing social and political order. He argues that it was this fear that helped increase support for the restoration* of the monarchy in 1660, proving the political power of Quakerism. In the foreword to the book, Hill says that Reay's work highlights "the importance of the revolutionary ambiance in which [the Quakers] originated" and that the work challenges the view that that "the rule of the gentry was somehow 'normal' and that the radicals were an insignificant minority."[2] In this way, Reay's work builds upon the picture of revolutionary turmoil and disruption that Hill had put forward.

During the 1980s, revisionist historians challenging some of the

> ❝ Hill was, however, not particularly preoccupied with studying the material 'infrastructure'. Instead, he rejoiced in the power of ideas—and particularly ideas generated within the tradition of radical Protestantism* that encouraged individuals to read their Bibles, to judge independently, and then to 'bear witness' to their beliefs, however unconventional. ❞
>
> Penelope J. Cornfield, 'We Are All One in the Eyes of the Lord'

Marxists' dominant claims and ways of working began to question Hill's main argument of a "revolt within the Revolution."[3] Some historians argued that it was anachronistic to apply the term "radicalism" to such activities, since the concept of radicalism had not even been invented at that point, while others argued that "radical" activity was actually much further from the mainstream than *The World Turned Upside Down* suggests.[4] For example, the historian of seventeenth-century Britain John Morrill,* while basically a defender of Hill's work, noted that "the limitations [of] his concentration on certain types of evidence … have become more evident as more and more sophisticated work has been attempted with new and unprinted sources."[5] Morrill thought that by using only printed sources Hill had misunderstood the nature of radical debate. He thought that later work, focusing on sources such as Church depositions and state records, had corrected this misunderstanding.

In his book *Fear, Myth and History: The Ranters and the Historians* (1986), the historian J. C. Davis* took this revisionism even further, arguing that one of Hill's groups, the Ranters,* never actually existed and that they were in fact a myth cooked up by conservative figures who wanted to strengthen the appeal of traditional values by coming up with an unattractive, extreme bogeyman. He also tried to expose the weakness of Hill's idea of a "revolt within the Revolution" by arguing that it is difficult to be sure who these revolutionaries actually were, and what it was they were trying to accomplish. This is because— as Hill himself admitted—the radicals were not a unified group and their aims and ambitions varied. For that very reason, Davis argues, it is impossible to see their actions as forming a joined "revolt within the Revolution."[6]

Schools of Thought

Hill was a Marxist historian and many elements of *The World Turned Upside Down* reflect his analytical approach, especially his insistence on social change from below. This argument depends on drawing a class-based line between the common people (the radicals) and the bourgeoisie.* Hill also tries to show how the specific socioeconomic circumstances of the common people contributed to the rise and spread of radical Puritan ideas.

Hill's work contributed to the Marxist school of history, then in vogue. He still had connections to the Communist Party Historians Group,* and the book fitted in with the group's aims of flagging up the radical and revolutionary spirit within the English consciousness.

In response to the popular current of Marxist analysis, a school of thought critical of Hill's theoretical position, the Revisionist School, developed. Hill's class-based model, for instance, was challenged by Gerald Aylmer* in his study of the origins of the Levellers,* which proved that it was difficult to work out whether the Levellers all belonged to the same socioeconomic group.[7] And the historian David Underdown* offered a study highlighting the existence of royalism (support for the crown) and traditionalism among the people—a challenge to Hill's lumping together of "radical" and "popular."[8]

In Current Scholarship

Hill's insistence on the importance of ideas, particularly the ideas of groups that had always been looked down on as the "lunatic fringe,"[9] still inspires scholars. He particularly wanted to highlight the fact that radical Puritanism was an important part of the English Revolution, claiming that it had a real social and political influence in the period, and so cannot be dismissed as marginal. In this way, *The World Turned Upside Down* can be seen as inspiring a field in history particularly concerned with the topic of radical Puritanism.

Historians who were interested in pursuing the significance of radical Puritanism even further include Barry Reay and William Lamont,* while more recently historians such as Ariel Hessayon* and Glenn Burgess* have tried to go deeper into the concept of "radicalism" to show how complex and multi-dimensional it was.

These studies challenge Hill's picture of radical Puritanism as a unified phenomenon that was the exclusive property of the common people. Instead, they set out to highlight both the differences between the radical groups and the ways in which educated clergymen and middle-class figures were involved in radical Puritanism. It is clear, however, that the ideas set out in *The World Turned Upside Down* served as a springboard for an investigation into these ideas. While these historians criticize Hill's methods and conclusions, they see how valuable the questions that Hill was asking about radical Puritanism were, and pursue these same questions themselves.

NOTES

1   Christopher Hill, *The World Turned Upside Down: Radical Ideas During the English Revolution* (London: Temple Smith, 1972, reprinted London: Penguin, 1991), 16.

2   Christopher Hill, "Foreword," in Barry Reay, *The Quakers and the English Revolution* (London: Temple Smith, 1985), vii–viii.

3   Hill, *World Turned Upside Down*, 14.

4   F. D. Dow, *Radicalism in the English Revolution 1640–1660* (Oxford: Blackwell, 1985), 1–9.

5   John Morrill, "Christopher Hill's Revolution," in *The Nature of the English Revolution: Essays by John Morrill*, ed. John Morrill (London: Longman, 1993), 279.

6   J. C. Davis, *Fear, Myth and History: The Ranters and the Historians* (Cambridge: Cambridge University Press, 1986), 133.

7   G. E. Aylmer, "Gentlemen Levellers?" in *The Intellectual Revolution of the Seventeenth Century*, ed. Charles Webster (London: Routledge, 1974), 103.

8   David Underdown, *Revel, Riot and Rebellion: Popular Politics and Culture in England 1603–1660* (Oxford: Clarendon Press, 1985).

9   Hill, *World Turned Upside Down*, 16.

MODULE 11
IMPACT AND INFLUENCE TODAY

KEY POINTS

- Hill's book is both a classic work of history and a text that scholars engage with as part of current debates over Puritanism* and revolution.
- Though scholars now tend to focus on individual radical* groups, Hill's model and arguments have remained influential.
- Scholars have questioned some of the broad assertions that Hill makes, such as the nature of "common people."

Position

Christopher Hill's picture of radical Puritanism as revolutionary in *The World Turned Upside Down: Radical Ideas During the English Revolution* is a classic piece of scholarship, and still inspires research today. In his 2000 study of the English Revolution* and how it fitted in with what was going on across Europe, the historian Jonathan Scott* declares, for example, that "English radicalism … *was* the English Revolution."[1] Though his critics—particularly the revisionists* of the 1980s—argued that Hill had made too much of radicalism, and the idea that all the various strands sat comfortably together, they did not completely do away with how important *The World Turned Upside Down* was. Scott even argues that this revolution was a "single fluid activity" because there was continuity between movements and they did share interests. He dismisses the idea that radicalism was split up into "discrete groups", and chooses to use the singular term "radical" to apply to all the movements as a whole.[2] This is in tune with Hill's desire to show how the radical Puritans shared common aims.

> ❝I was raised on Christopher Hill and remain inspired by his works.❞
>
> Stevie Davies, *Unbridled Spirits: Women of the English Revolution, 1640–1660*

Hill's idea that there were in fact "two revolutions," one that propped up the rights of the ruling classes, and another that threatened to overturn them, is still important to studies of the English Revolution today. The early modern* historian Michael Braddick's* *God's Fury, England's Fire* (2008) focuses on the "creative and radical politics" that emerged in revolutionary England. He sets out to show the sheer scale of the ideological upheavals and conflicting political and social agendas that were making themselves felt as the constitutional crisis raged.[3]

Braddick, like Hill, wanted to look beyond the conflict between the king and Parliament: "It is conventional to tell that constitutional story—of a republican* failure ending in restoration*—but to do so is to limit the significance of the 1640s to that single constitutional question. There is much more to say, and to remember, about England's decade of civil war and revolution. Political and religious questions of fundamental importance were thrashed out before broad political audiences as activists and opportunists sought to mobilize support for their proposals."[4]

In fact, Braddick calls *The World Turned Upside Down* the "classic" study of radical Puritan political activity and "religious experimentation."[5] It is a classic because, as the political historian Glenn Burgess* has pointed out, *The World Turned Upside Down* is still the only work to offer a complete and comprehensive account of Puritan radicalism. Other works may have found problems with Hill's idea of a "revolt within the Revolution,"[6] but they have not come up with anything that presents a complete alternative picture of the origins, nature, and effects of Puritan radicalism.[7]

Interaction

The World Turned Upside Down was instrumental in bringing the debate over the nature and extent of English radicalism back to the table. Recent studies, such as *Treacherous Faith* (2013) by professor of English David Loewenstein*, follow Hill in underlining the power of "early modern religious phobias, especially as they were generated by the perception of unorthodox beliefs and their practitioners and expressed in literary culture."[8] Loewenstein tries to take seriously the radical beliefs that he outlines; this owes much to *The World Turned Upside Down*, and other work by Hill, especially in the way it prioritizes printed and literary sources. Using the same method of study as Hill, Loewenstein shows the potential of the heretical (radically unorthodox) beliefs he talks about, and the effect these heresies had on those heresy-hunters who occupied positions of power. The fact that he is sympathetic to the radicals is also in tune with Hill.

Many historians today have tried to move away from Hill's monolithic picture of revolutionary radical Puritanism—or even English radicalism. They have tended to adopt a "functional" approach that gives more importance to the specific contexts and features of each movement instead.[9] As the historians of ideas Ariel Hessayon* and David Finnegan* say, historians do not deny "radicalism's usefulness as an explanatory category in scholarly discussions of the early modern period," but they insist on "the need for sensitivity to context and consequently the situational, episodic and variegated nature of radicalism."[10] They are arguing against Hill's idea that there was one united radical movement.

The Continuing Debate

Many scholars have tried to resist Hill's lumping together of radical groups in *The World Turned Upside Down*. An example of this is Hessayon's in-depth study of the radical preacher Theaurau John Tany.* What Hessayon set out to do in writing this book was to present a totally objective picture of Tany's activities and writings. To this end, he does not bring any wider context or historical significance to the discussion—a vision of the history of radical Puritanism quite contrary to that put forward in *The World Turned Upside Down*. Hessayon also argues that, by looking closely at TheaurauJohn Tany's works and the origins and context of his ideas, a number of problems with *The World Turned Upside Down* crop up, including the fact that Hill "used evidence selectively to fit his theories."[11]

Hill's equation of radical Puritanism with the common people is another aspect of his work now being questioned. For example, in *The English Radical Imagination* (2003), the professor of early modern literature Nicholas McDowell* points out that many of the authors of radical Puritan texts "possessed a considerable degree of formal education."[12] Richard Overton,* a Leveller,* and Isaac Pennington,* a Quaker,* both went to Cambridge University and produced work that promoted the ideas and beliefs of their respective movements. McDowell argues that representing radical Puritanism as exclusively popular is not quite as clear cut as *The World Turned Upside Down* suggests. This also serves to challenge the idea of "a revolt within the Revolution," since this is an idea that relies on the conflict between the "common" radicals and the conservative middle class; not all radicals, McDowell shows, can be considered as "common."

NOTES

1   Jonathan Scott, *England's Troubles: Seventeenth-Century English Political Instability in European Context* (Cambridge: Cambridge University Press, 2000), 35.

2   Scott, *England's Troubles*, 320.

3   Michael Braddick, *God's Fury, England's Fire: A New History of the English Civil Wars* (London: Penguin, 2009), xxvi.

4   Braddick, *God's Fury*, xxv.

5   Braddick, *God's Fury*, 655, 673.

6   Christopher Hill, *The World Turned Upside Down: Radical Ideas During the English Revolution* (London: Temple Smith, 1972, reprinted London: Penguin, 1991), 14.

7   Glenn Burgess, "Radicalism and the English Revolution," in *English Radicalism, 1550–1850*, ed. Glenn Burgess and Matthew Festenstein (Cambridge: Cambridge University Press, 2007), 62.

8   David Loewenstein, *Treacherous Faith: The Specter of Heresy in Early Modern English Literature and Culture* (Oxford: Oxford University Press, 2013), 1.

9   Glenn Burgess, "A Matter of Context: 'Radicalism' and the English Revolution," in *Cromohs Virtual Seminars: Recent Historiographical Trends of the British Studies (17th–18th Centuries)*, 2006–7: 1–4, accessed March 12, 2014, http://www.cromohs.unifi.it/seminari/burgess_radicalism.html.

10 Ariel Hessayon and David Finnegan, "Introduction," in *Varieties of Seventeenth- and Early Eighteenth-Century English Radicalism in Context*, ed. Ariel Hessayon and David Finnegan (Farnham: Ashgate, 2011), 25.

11 Ariel Hessayon, *"Gold Tried in the Fire": The Prophet TheaurauJohn Tany and the English Revolution* (Aldershot: Ashgate, 2007), 8.

12 Nicholas McDowell, *The English Radical Imagination: Culture, Religion, and Revolution, 1630–1660* (Oxford: Oxford University Press, 2003), 6.

MODULE 12
WHERE NEXT?

KEY POINTS

- *The World Turned Upside Down* is a classic piece of historical work, and a valuable starting point for scholarship at many different levels.
- Although they have updated them, scholars are still working on the ideas, concepts, and analytical frameworks that Hill generated.
- Hill's work offers a comprehensive analysis of radicalism* that has not yet been surpassed.

Potential

Christopher Hill's *The World Turned Upside Down* is without doubt a classic history of the English Revolution.* It is also a prominent example of the values of Marxist* history. It established the importance of revolutionary radical Puritanism* and the reasons why it was credible as an area of serious academic study.

In the years since *The World Turned Upside Down* was published, historians have attacked and developed its ideas. But even if we take on board that there are problems with the work, in many ways it is still the single, authoritative text on Puritan radicalism as a whole. Even though people have questioned the way Hill paints his picture of radicalism, his text has not been replaced. Indeed, although some of Hill's conclusions have been challenged in the past 40 years, his book raised questions that historians are still attempting to answer today.

Serving as a starting point for anyone wishing to investigate the role of English Puritan radicalism during the seventeenth century, and for anyone who wants to understand the relationship between ideas,

> ❝ We may be too conditioned by the way up the world has been for the last three hundred years to be fair to those in the seventeenth century who saw other possibilities. But we should try. ❞
>
> Christopher Hill, *The World Turned Upside Down: Radical Ideas During the English Revolution*

politics, religion, and socioeconomic circumstances, *The World Turned Upside Down* will no doubt be influential for some time to come.

Future Directions

The World Turned Upside Down is likely to continue to be important for historians of the English Revolution, and they still engage with the text in new and revealing ways today. While there is no single scholar whom one could say is an "heir to Hill," historians of the period in general owe a lot to the pioneering work he did, which now provides a background and a springboard for a wide variety of work on English radicalism.

Current historians interested in the history of radical Puritanism see that "[we] still lack a post-revisionist* view that is as comprehensive as Hill's."[1] That is, the picture of radical Puritanism presented in *The World Turned Upside Down* is still the best and most comprehensive picture of Puritan radicalism that historians have. So it is with this text, and the issues it brings up, that historians have to engage. More and more they do this with micro-histories (studies of very specific events, individuals, or phenomena) of particular radical groups studied by Hill, rather than attempting a comprehensive overview of radicalism. An example is the historian John Gurney's* study of the Diggers*.[2]

The World Turned Upside Down has also become an important piece of history in its own right. It is a part of a long tradition in the study of history. In his recent book on the history of biblical studies, James

Crossley,* a professor of the ways in which the Bible has been used for political purposes, gives an entire chapter to Hill's understanding of the Bible in radical culture. Not only does he stress the importance of *The World Turned Upside Down*, but he also shows how its political arguments can be used in other fields of study. He writes that "we could make the argument that Hill's reading of radical scholarly biblical interpretation" was "akin to their political contribution to historical development: bourgeois* biblical interpretation may have won in the long run but not without the mark of popular radical interpretation."[3]

Summary

The World Turned Upside Down is still an important text in the study of the English Revolution, and of the subject of radical thought more broadly. It not only offers a lively and accessible overview of the groups involved in the revolution and what came after, but also is a prime example of Marxist historiography*—the way Marxist historians have written about history. Though some of its claims and ideas have been revised, by both the author and those who criticized the work, it is still a crucial account of radical history, and without reading Hill's work it will be much harder to understand current studies of the subject.

Hill's concept of a "revolt within the Revolution"[4] was a breakthrough. This began the process of rehabilitating the "lunatic fringe"[5] who had been, and perhaps still are, overlooked by historians focusing on the outcomes of the English Civil Wars.* He also demonstrated the power of ideas to influence events; even if those radical plans of action were ultimately unsuccessful, Hill was able to show that they had an impact on the ideologies that did become dominant after the revolution.

The breadth and depth of material covered by the book guarantees its continuing appeal. There has not been another survey of radicalism as wide ranging as Hill's, and given the trends towards smaller histories of individuals or groups, it looks as if it will remain the most comprehensive analysis of radicalism for some time yet. Although *The World Turned Upside Down* has been expanded, critiqued, and complicated by the studies that have followed it, it remains a text that holds a powerful influence over its field.

NOTES

1   Glenn Burgess, "Radicalism and the English Revolution," in *English Radicalism, 1550–1850*, ed. Glenn Burgess and Matthew Festenstein (Cambridge: Cambridge University Press, 2007), 64.

2   John Gurney, *Brave Community: The Digger Movement in the English Revolution* (Manchester: Manchester University Press, 2007).

3   James G. Crossley, *Harnessing Chaos: The Bible in English Political Discourse since 1968* (London: Bloomsbury, 2014), 59.

4   Christopher Hill, *The World Turned Upside Down: Radical Ideas During the English Revolution* (London: Temple Smith, 1972, reprinted London: Penguin, 1991), 14.

5   Hill, *World Turned Upside Down*, 16.

GLOSSARY

GLOSSARY OF TERMS

Annales School: a school of historical research and analysis that emphasizes long-term (*longue durée*) trends and changes in society. The school is named after its journal, *Annales d'histoire économique et sociale*, which was founded by the French historians Marc Bloch and Lucien Febvre in 1929.

Antinomianism: literally, "against the law." An extreme version of the belief that mankind is saved by faith alone, which justifies the rejection of any kind of moral restriction on one's behavior.

Aristocracy: members of the highest or upper class of society. In seventeenth-century England, this class was composed of those with titles, land holdings, and so on, inherited by birth.

Bourgeoisie: in Marxist theory, this is the group of people who have access to capital and therefore are able to monopolize production. They tend to have an interest in securing the rights of money and property.

Capitalism: an economic system in which private ownership controls a country's trade and industry, with the aim of producing a profit.

Cold War (1947–91): a period of tension between the capitalist United States and the communism Soviet Union, which sidestepped direct military conflict in favor of espionage and proxy wars.

Communism: a political theory that aims for the creation of a classless society based upon common ownership of the means of production—tools, factories, and resources—and property.

Communist Party Historians Group: a group of Marxist academics founded in 1946. It produced a number of studies in social and economic history until 1991, when it transformed into the Socialist History Society.

Constitutionalism: the idea that government is subject to, and its power limited by, the law. In the case of the English Civil Wars, it was a matter of Parliament attempting to restrict the powers of the king.

Diggers: a radical group that sought to create egalitarian agricultural communities by cultivating common land during the English Civil Wars.

Early modern: a period of European history generally accepted to begin in the late fifteenth century and end in the last decades of the eighteenth century.

Egalitarian: a belief in the principle that everyone should be equal in status, without discrimination by birth, race, or gender.

English Civil Wars: a series of wars, 1642–51, between King Charles I and (after his execution) royalist supporters on the one side and the English Parliament (sometimes known as the Long Parliament, because it sat from 1640 to 1648) on the other. There were many causes for the war, but the primary dispute was over the extent of royal power.

English Revolution: a period covering the English Civil Wars between the king and Parliament and the decade of republican government that followed. During the years 1640–60, owing to the war and collapse of censorship, a whole range of radical views could be expressed more freely than before or after.

Feminism: a broad social movement dedicated to furthering the rights of women. There is no single "feminist" movement; rather, lots of movements and groups with different aims (such as equal pay or access to education) can come under the banner of feminism.

Feudalism: the predominant social system in medieval Europe, characterized by relationships based around either land ownership or labor in the service of landowners.

Great Depression: a severe economic downturn in the 1930s to the 1940s that affected many industrialized countries across the world.

Historiography: the study of historical criticism, including methodological innovation and the development of the discipline as a whole.

Levellers: a radical movement that emerged during the English Revolution. They called for popular voting and religious toleration.

Marxism: an analytical model that sees class conflict, and economic conflict more broadly, as the cause of social and cultural change.

Methodist: a follower of the Methodist Church—a denomination of the Protestant Church co-founded by the English religious reformer John Wesley in the eighteenth century.

New Model Army: a professional army formed by Parliament in 1645. Many of the soldiers had radical political or religious convictions that led them to fight for Parliament.

Popular sovereignty: the principle that the people are the source of political power. The people may grant their power to government, but as the source of power in a country they are able to change a government when they wish.

Protestant: a follower of the Protestant Church: one of the two major branches of the Christian faith, which broke from Roman Catholicism in the sixteenth century.

Protestant ethic: an idea developed by the influential German social theorist Max Weber in his 1904 book *The Protestant Ethic and the Spirit of Capitalism.* Weber argued that Protestantism was used to encourage productive work and the accumulation of wealth and property, which became the basis of European capitalism.

Puritans: a group of Protestants who argued that the Roman Catholic faith was too influential, and sought to purify their church. For Hill, Puritanism does not always signify a particular group, but covers a range of religious radical positions.

Quakers: a religious movement founded by George Fox (1624–91) in the late 1640s that emphasized the personal, internal experience of God over external teachings.

Radical: in the context of political history, "radical" ideas and groups are those founded on a desire for fundamental social reform, generally through revolutionary change.

Ranters: an antinomian sect who believed that moral law had no hold over them and who promoted the pantheistic idea of God within everyone and everything.

Republican: one who supports government by the people, usually through elected representatives, rather than hereditary rule (monarchy) or rule by an individual with absolute power (despotism).

Restoration: the return of Charles II as king in 1660, after 11 years of republican rule.

Revisionism: when a historian challenges an existing interpretation of a historical event on the basis of new information or a unique analysis of existing materials.

Socialism: a political and social theory, closely linked to communism, which advocates collective control of industry and communal land ownership. The movement often involves the setting up of co-operative groups to bring about such a state.

Social theory: the attempt to explain social phenomena through the application of various analytical frameworks.

Soviet Union: the Union of Soviet Socialist Republics (USSR; Russian CCCP) was an international union of socialist states, led by modern-day Russia. The states in the union were at best semi-independent, with economies and societies controlled centrally from Moscow.

Wall Street Crash: an economic crisis of the early twentieth century; between October 28 and 29, 1929, the US stock market lost about $30 billion in value as stock prices plummeted, resulting in the Great Depression.

World War II: a global conflict that took place between 1939 and 1945. The primary combatants were the Allied powers (the United States, the UK, and France) and the Axis powers (Germany, Italy, and Japan).

PEOPLE MENTIONED IN THE TEXT

G. E. Aylmer (1926–2000) was a social and economic historian. He was a PhD student of Christopher Hill, interested in the nature of early modern bureaucracy in the build-up to, and during, the English Revolution.

Michael Braddick (b. 1962) is a historian of the early modern period. Like Hill, he focuses on the radical generation of ideas, which he sees as important to the development of science and politics in the eighteenth century and beyond.

Glenn Burgess (b. 1961) is a political historian, currently a professor and pro-vice chancellor at the University of Hull. He has published extensively on radical political thought.

Bernard Capp is a professor emeritus at the University of Warwick. He has published widely on the radical groups of the English Revolution.

Charles I (1600–49) was king of England in the build-up to the English Civil Wars. He argued that kings had the divine right to rule without consultation with their subjects, a position that brought him into conflict with Parliament. He was executed for tyranny in 1649.

Charles II (1630–85) was the son of Charles I. After fleeing to France on the execution of his father in 1649, he was invited to return to England as king in 1660, ending the republic. His reign is dated from 1649, although he was not technically crowned king until 1660.

James Crossley is a professor of the Bible, culture, and politics at the University of Sheffield. His work focuses on the way religion is used in particular social contexts, including the use of the Bible for radical ends.

J. C. Davis is a historian who specializes in the leaders of the English Revolution, though he has also written extensively on the Ranters.

David Finnegan is a historian of ideas, whose work investigates the nature of the "radical tradition" in English culture.

George Fox (1624–91) was born in Leicestershire and became a preacher in London, and later the North American colonies. He was the founder of the Quaker movement.

Samuel Rawson Gardiner (1829–1902) was an early historian of the English Revolution. His conception of the period as a "Puritan Revolution," which challenged the power of the Church of England and paved the way for religious freedom, was hugely influential until it was challenged by Hill.

John Gurney (1960–2014) was a historian of the Digger movement.

Ariel Hessayon is a historian of radicals and radical ideas during the English Revolution, best known for his biography of the eccentric radical TheaurauJohn Tany.

J. H. Hexter (1910–96) was a historian of seventeenth-century Britain. His reputation comes primarily from his interventions in historiography, especially his debate with Hill over the nature and use of historical sources.

Rodney Hilton (1916–2002) was an English historian. A Marxist, he is noted for his work dealing with the late medieval period and the transition from the social system of feudalism to that of capitalism.

William Lamont is emeritus professor of history at Sussex University; a historian of early modern England, his specialism is the Ranters.

David Loewenstein (b. 1955) is professor of English at Penn State University. He has published on a wide variety of early modern literary works and their connection to the radical ideas of their day.

Phyllis Mack is a historian of early modern women and popular religion.

Soma Marik is a Marxist historian who has helped to develop Hill's work by expanding the scope of enquiry to radical women.

Karl Marx (1818–83) was born in Prussia (modern-day Germany) but spent much of his life in England. He produced a number of analyses of capitalism. He argued that the inherent tensions between labor and capital would lead to the overthrow of capitalism, and its replacement by a socialist economic model.

Nicholas McDowell is professor of early modern literature at the University of Exeter. He has written on the radical imagination, as well as on the impact of radical thought on the literature and culture of early modern England.

Frank McGregor was a student of Christopher Hill. After submitting his thesis in 1968, he published extensively on the Ranters and other radical sects.

George Monck (1608–70) was a general in the New Model Army. He was instrumental in securing the return of Charles II, and was made duke of Albemarle in return, in 1660.

John Morrill (b. 1946) is a historian of seventeenth-century England. He especially focuses on the countryside, and its relationship to the politics and ideas of the state as a whole.

A. L. Morton (1903–87) was a prominent Marxist historian and chair of the Communist Party Historians Group, who published a study of the Ranters.

James Nayler (1616–60) was an early convert to the Quaker movement. He provoked controversy in 1656 by riding into Bristol on a donkey, imitating Christ; he was arrested and tried for blasphemy.

Richard Overton (1599–1664) was a preacher and printer, best known for his scathing attacks on bishops and the doctrine that the soul dies with the body and is resurrected at the Last Judgment.

Isaac Pennington (1616–79) was an early convert to the Quaker movement. He wrote on a wide range of issues central to the cause, and was imprisoned frequently for his writings.

John Pym (1584–1643) was an important Parliamentarian and opponent of Charles I. Charles I attempted to arrest him in the Parliament buildings in 1642, an act which helped spark the English Civil Wars.

Barry Reay is a historian of rural cultures and beliefs, including the radical cultures found among farm workers.

Jonathan Scott is professor of history at the University of Auckland. His work focuses on political history and the history of ideas, especially during the English Civil Wars.

Lawrence Stone (1919–99) was a social historian who helped begin the debate over the wealth and power of the aristocracy in the lead-up to the English Revolution.

TheaurauJohn Tany (1608–59) was a goldsmith who became a self-proclaimed prophet in his thirties. He published several mystical works. Christopher Hill describes him as "probably ... mad."

Joan Thirsk (1922–2013) was a social historian, specializing in the development of agriculture. As well as writing a number of detailed studies of farming and food culture, she helped to popularize the use of local sources and manuscripts in wider historical studies.

Keith Thomas (b. 1933) is a social historian whose work helped to popularize the study of "history from below." His publications focus on popular belief and the spread of radical or revolutionary ideas in early modern England.

E. P. Thompson (1924–93) was a Marxist historian whose work focused on the development of the working class during the eighteenth and nineteenth centuries.

David Underdown (1925–2009) was a student of Christopher Hill. He wrote a number of studies of royalists and royalism during the English Civil Wars.

Max Weber (1864–1920) was a German social theorist, primarily concerned with understanding how individuals rationalized their decisions. His conception of the Protestant ethic was fundamental to Hill's understanding of the development of English society.

Gerrard Winstanley (1609–76) was the founder and leader of the Digger movement. He published a number of pamphlets arguing for the redistribution and shared usage of land.

WORKS CITED

WORKS CITED

Aylmer, G. E. "Gentlemen Levellers?" In *The Intellectual Revolution of the Seventeenth Century*, edited by Charles Webster, 101–8. London: Routledge, 1974.

Braddick, Michael. *God's Fury, England's Fire: A New History of the English Civil Wars*. London: Penguin, 2009.

Burgess, Glenn. "Radicalism and the English Revolution." In *English Radicalism, 1550–1850*, edited by Glenn Burgess and Matthew Festenstein, 62–86. Cambridge: Cambridge University Press, 2007.

_____. "A Matter of Context: 'Radicalism' and the English Revolution." In *Cromohs Virtual Seminars: Recent Historiographical Trends of the British Studies (17th–18th Centuries)*, 2006–7: 1–4. Accessed March 12, 2014. http://www.cromohs.unifi.it/seminari/burgess_radicalism.html.

Capp, Bernard. "The Fifth Monarchists and Popular Millenarianism." In *Radical Religion in the English Revolution*, edited by J. F. McGregor and Barry Reay, 165–89. Oxford: Oxford University Press, 1984.

Corfield, Penelope J. "'We Are All One in the Eyes of the Lord': Christopher Hill and the Historical Meanings of Radical Religion." *History Workshop Journal* 58 (2004): 110–27.

Crossley, James G. *Harnessing Chaos: The Bible in English Political Discourse since 1968*. London: Bloomsbury, 2014.

Davis, J. C. *Fear, Myth and History: The Ranters and the Historians*. Cambridge: Cambridge University Press, 1986.

Dow, F. D. *Radicalism in the English Revolution 1640–1660*. Oxford: Blackwell, 1985.

Dunn, John. "'Triggers and Diggers.'" *Listener*, August 3, 1972.

Elias, Amy J. *Sublime Desire: History and Post-1960s Fiction*. Baltimore, MD: Johns Hopkins University Press, 2001.

Gurney, John. *Brave Community: The Digger Movement in the English Revolution*. Manchester: Manchester University Press, 2007.

Hessayon, Ariel. *"Gold Tried in the Fire": The Prophet TheaurauJohn Tany and the English Revolution*. Aldershot: Ashgate, 2007.

Hessayon, Ariel, and David Finnegan. "Introduction." In *Varieties of Seventeenth- and Early Eighteenth-Century English Radicalism in Context*, edited by Ariel Hessayon and David Finnegan, 1–29. Farnham: Ashgate, 2011.

Hexter, J. H. "Christopher Hill: The Burden of Proof," *Times Literary Supplement*, October 24, 1975.

Hill, Christopher. *The World Turned Upside Down: Radical Ideas During the English Revolution.* London: Temple Smith, 1972, reprinted London: Penguin, 1991.

_____. *Change and Continuity in Seventeenth-Century England.* Cambridge, MA: Harvard University Press, 1975.

_____. "Reply to Hexter." *Times Literary Supplement*, November 7, 1975.

_____. "Foreword." In Barry Reay, *The Quakers and the English Revolution*. London: Temple Smith, 1985.

_____. "Talking with Christopher Hill: Part I." In *Reviving the English Revolution: Reflections and Elaborations on the Work of Christopher Hill*, edited by Geoff Eley and William Hunt, 99–103. London: Verso: 1988.

Loewenstein, David. *Treacherous Faith: The Specter of Heresy in Early Modern English Literature and Culture*. Oxford: Oxford University Press, 2013.

Mack, Phyllis. "The Prophet and Her Audience: Gender and Knowledge in *The World Turned Upside Down*." In *Reviving the English Revolution: Reflections and Elaborations on the Work of Christopher Hill*, edited by Geoff Eley and William Hunt, 139–52. London: Verso: 1988.

Marik, Soma. "Christopher Hill: Women Turning the World Upside Down." *Social Scientist* 32, no. 3/4 (2004): 50–70.

McDowell, Nicholas. *The English Radical Imagination: Culture, Religion, and Revolution, 1630–1660*. Oxford: Oxford University Press, 2003.

McGregor, J. F. "The Ranters, 1649–1660." B. Litt thesis, Oxford University, 1968.

Morrill, John. "Christopher Hill's Revolution." In *The Nature of the English Revolution: Essays by John Morrill*, edited by John Morrill, 273–84. London: Longman, 1993.

Morton, A. L. *The World of the Ranters: Religious Radicalism in the English Revolution*. London: Lawrence and Wishart, 1970.

Richardson, R. C. *The Debate on the English Revolution*. Manchester: Manchester University Press, 1998.

Scott, Jonathan. *England's Troubles: Seventeenth-Century English Political Instability in European Context*. Cambridge: Cambridge University Press, 2000.

Thomas, Keith. *Religion and the Decline of Magic: Studies in Popular Beliefs in Sixteenth- and Seventeenth-Century England.* New York: Charles Scribner's Sons, 1971.

Thompson, E. P. *The Making of the English Working Class*. London: Victor Gollancz, 1963.

Trueman, Carl R. *Histories and Fallacies: Problems Faced in the Writing of History*. Wheaton, IL: Crossway, 2010.

Underdown, David. *Pride's Purge*. Oxford: Oxford University Press, 1971.

_____. *Revel, Riot and Rebellion: Popular Politics and Culture in England 1603–1660*. Oxford: Clarendon Press, 1985.

Woolrych, Austin. Review of *The World Turned Upside Down* by Christopher Hill. *History* 58 (1973): 290.

THE MACAT LIBRARY
BY DISCIPLINE

AFRICANA STUDIES

Chinua Achebe's *An Image of Africa: Racism in Conrad's Heart of Darkness*
W. E. B. Du Bois's *The Souls of Black Folk*
Zora Neale Huston's *Characteristics of Negro Expression*
Martin Luther King Jr's *Why We Can't Wait*
Toni Morrison's *Playing in the Dark: Whiteness in the American Literary Imagination*

ANTHROPOLOGY

Arjun Appadurai's *Modernity at Large: Cultural Dimensions of Globalisation*
Philippe Ariès's *Centuries of Childhood*
Franz Boas's *Race, Language and Culture*
Kim Chan & Renée Mauborgne's *Blue Ocean Strategy*
Jared Diamond's *Guns, Germs & Steel: the Fate of Human Societies*
Jared Diamond's *Collapse: How Societies Choose to Fail or Survive*
E. E. Evans-Pritchard's *Witchcraft, Oracles and Magic Among the Azande*
James Ferguson's *The Anti-Politics Machine*
Clifford Geertz's *The Interpretation of Cultures*
David Graeber's *Debt: the First 5000 Years*
Karen Ho's *Liquidated: An Ethnography of Wall Street*
Geert Hofstede's *Culture's Consequences: Comparing Values, Behaviors, Institutes and Organizations across Nations*
Claude Lévi-Strauss's *Structural Anthropology*
Jay Macleod's *Ain't No Makin' It: Aspirations and Attainment in a Low-Income Neighborhood*
Saba Mahmood's *The Politics of Piety: The Islamic Revival and the Feminist Subject*
Marcel Mauss's *The Gift*

BUSINESS

Jean Lave & Etienne Wenger's *Situated Learning*
Theodore Levitt's *Marketing Myopia*
Burton G. Malkiel's *A Random Walk Down Wall Street*
Douglas McGregor's *The Human Side of Enterprise*
Michael Porter's *Competitive Strategy: Creating and Sustaining Superior Performance*
John Kotter's *Leading Change*
C. K. Prahalad & Gary Hamel's *The Core Competence of the Corporation*

CRIMINOLOGY

Michelle Alexander's *The New Jim Crow: Mass Incarceration in the Age of Colorblindness*
Michael R. Gottfredson & Travis Hirschi's *A General Theory of Crime*
Richard Herrnstein & Charles A. Murray's *The Bell Curve: Intelligence and Class Structure in American Life*
Elizabeth Loftus's *Eyewitness Testimony*
Jay Macleod's *Ain't No Makin' It: Aspirations and Attainment in a Low-Income Neighborhood*
Philip Zimbardo's *The Lucifer Effect*

ECONOMICS

Janet Abu-Lughod's *Before European Hegemony*
Ha-Joon Chang's *Kicking Away the Ladder*
David Brion Davis's *The Problem of Slavery in the Age of Revolution*
Milton Friedman's *The Role of Monetary Policy*
Milton Friedman's *Capitalism and Freedom*
David Graeber's *Debt: the First 5000 Years*
Friedrich Hayek's *The Road to Serfdom*
Karen Ho's *Liquidated: An Ethnography of Wall Street*

John Maynard Keynes's *The General Theory of Employment, Interest and Money*
Charles P. Kindleberger's *Manias, Panics and Crashes*
Robert Lucas's *Why Doesn't Capital Flow from Rich to Poor Countries?*
Burton G. Malkiel's *A Random Walk Down Wall Street*
Thomas Robert Malthus's *An Essay on the Principle of Population*
Karl Marx's *Capital*
Thomas Piketty's *Capital in the Twenty-First Century*
Amartya Sen's *Development as Freedom*
Adam Smith's *The Wealth of Nations*
Nassim Nicholas Taleb's *The Black Swan: The Impact of the Highly Improbable*
Amos Tversky's & Daniel Kahneman's *Judgment under Uncertainty: Heuristics and Biases*
Mahbub Ul Haq's *Reflections on Human Development*
Max Weber's *The Protestant Ethic and the Spirit of Capitalism*

FEMINISM AND GENDER STUDIES

Judith Butler's *Gender Trouble*
Simone De Beauvoir's *The Second Sex*
Michel Foucault's *History of Sexuality*
Betty Friedan's *The Feminine Mystique*
Saba Mahmood's *The Politics of Piety: The Islamic Revival and the Feminist Subject*
Joan Wallach Scott's *Gender and the Politics of History*
Mary Wollstonecraft's *A Vindication of the Rights of Women*
Virginia Woolf's *A Room of One's Own*

GEOGRAPHY

The Brundtland Report's *Our Common Future*
Rachel Carson's *Silent Spring*
Charles Darwin's *On the Origin of Species*
James Ferguson's *The Anti-Politics Machine*
Jane Jacobs's *The Death and Life of Great American Cities*
James Lovelock's *Gaia: A New Look at Life on Earth*
Amartya Sen's *Development as Freedom*
Mathis Wackernagel & William Rees's *Our Ecological Footprint*

HISTORY

Janet Abu-Lughod's *Before European Hegemony*
Benedict Anderson's *Imagined Communities*
Bernard Bailyn's *The Ideological Origins of the American Revolution*
Hanna Batatu's *The Old Social Classes And The Revolutionary Movements Of Iraq*
Christopher Browning's *Ordinary Men: Reserve Police Batallion 101 and the Final Solution in Poland*
Edmund Burke's *Reflections on the Revolution in France*
William Cronon's *Nature's Metropolis: Chicago And The Great West*
Alfred W. Crosby's *The Columbian Exchange*
Hamid Dabashi's *Iran: A People Interrupted*
David Brion Davis's *The Problem of Slavery in the Age of Revolution*
Nathalie Zemon Davis's *The Return of Martin Guerre*
Jared Diamond's *Guns, Germs & Steel: the Fate of Human Societies*
Frank Dikotter's *Mao's Great Famine*
John W Dower's *War Without Mercy: Race And Power In The Pacific War*
W. E. B. Du Bois's *The Souls of Black Folk*
Richard J. Evans's *In Defence of History*
Lucien Febvre's *The Problem of Unbelief in the 16th Century*
Sheila Fitzpatrick's *Everyday Stalinism*

Eric Foner's *Reconstruction: America's Unfinished Revolution, 1863-1877*
Michel Foucault's *Discipline and Punish*
Michel Foucault's *History of Sexuality*
Francis Fukuyama's *The End of History and the Last Man*
John Lewis Gaddis's *We Now Know: Rethinking Cold War History*
Ernest Gellner's *Nations and Nationalism*
Eugene Genovese's *Roll, Jordan, Roll: The World the Slaves Made*
Carlo Ginzburg's *The Night Battles*
Daniel Goldhagen's *Hitler's Willing Executioners*
Jack Goldstone's *Revolution and Rebellion in the Early Modern World*
Antonio Gramsci's *The Prison Notebooks*
Alexander Hamilton, John Jay & James Madison's *The Federalist Papers*
Christopher Hill's *The World Turned Upside Down*
Carole Hillenbrand's *The Crusades: Islamic Perspectives*
Thomas Hobbes's *Leviathan*
Eric Hobsbawm's *The Age Of Revolution*
John A. Hobson's *Imperialism: A Study*
Albert Hourani's *History of the Arab Peoples*
Samuel P. Huntington's *The Clash of Civilizations and the Remaking of World Order*
C. L. R. James's *The Black Jacobins*
Tony Judt's *Postwar: A History of Europe Since 1945*
Ernst Kantorowicz's *The King's Two Bodies: A Study in Medieval Political Theology*
Paul Kennedy's *The Rise and Fall of the Great Powers*
Ian Kershaw's *The "Hitler Myth": Image and Reality in the Third Reich*
John Maynard Keynes's *The General Theory of Employment, Interest and Money*
Charles P. Kindleberger's *Manias, Panics and Crashes*
Martin Luther King Jr's *Why We Can't Wait*
Henry Kissinger's *World Order: Reflections on the Character of Nations and the Course of History*
Thomas Kuhn's *The Structure of Scientific Revolutions*
Georges Lefebvre's *The Coming of the French Revolution*
John Locke's *Two Treatises of Government*
Niccolò Machiavelli's *The Prince*
Thomas Robert Malthus's *An Essay on the Principle of Population*
Mahmood Mamdani's *Citizen and Subject: Contemporary Africa And The Legacy Of Late Colonialism*
Karl Marx's *Capital*
Stanley Milgram's *Obedience to Authority*
John Stuart Mill's *On Liberty*
Thomas Paine's *Common Sense*
Thomas Paine's *Rights of Man*
Geoffrey Parker's *Global Crisis: War, Climate Change and Catastrophe in the Seventeenth Century*
Jonathan Riley-Smith's *The First Crusade and the Idea of Crusading*
Jean-Jacques Rousseau's *The Social Contract*
Joan Wallach Scott's *Gender and the Politics of History*
Theda Skocpol's *States and Social Revolutions*
Adam Smith's *The Wealth of Nations*
Timothy Snyder's *Bloodlands: Europe Between Hitler and Stalin*
Sun Tzu's *The Art of War*
Keith Thomas's *Religion and the Decline of Magic*
Thucydides's *The History of the Peloponnesian War*
Frederick Jackson Turner's *The Significance of the Frontier in American History*
Odd Arne Westad's *The Global Cold War: Third World Interventions And The Making Of Our Times*

LITERATURE

Chinua Achebe's *An Image of Africa: Racism in Conrad's Heart of Darkness*
Roland Barthes's *Mythologies*
Homi K. Bhabha's *The Location of Culture*
Judith Butler's *Gender Trouble*
Simone De Beauvoir's *The Second Sex*
Ferdinand De Saussure's *Course in General Linguistics*
T. S. Eliot's *The Sacred Wood: Essays on Poetry and Criticism*
Zora Neale Huston's *Characteristics of Negro Expression*
Toni Morrison's *Playing in the Dark: Whiteness in the American Literary Imagination*
Edward Said's *Orientalism*
Gayatri Chakravorty Spivak's *Can the Subaltern Speak?*
Mary Wollstonecraft's *A Vindication of the Rights of Women*
Virginia Woolf's *A Room of One's Own*

PHILOSOPHY

Elizabeth Anscombe's *Modern Moral Philosophy*
Hannah Arendt's *The Human Condition*
Aristotle's *Metaphysics*
Aristotle's *Nicomachean Ethics*
Edmund Gettier's *Is Justified True Belief Knowledge?*
Georg Wilhelm Friedrich Hegel's *Phenomenology of Spirit*
David Hume's *Dialogues Concerning Natural Religion*
David Hume's *The Enquiry for Human Understanding*
Immanuel Kant's *Religion within the Boundaries of Mere Reason*
Immanuel Kant's *Critique of Pure Reason*
Søren Kierkegaard's *The Sickness Unto Death*
Søren Kierkegaard's *Fear and Trembling*
C. S. Lewis's *The Abolition of Man*
Alasdair MacIntyre's *After Virtue*
Marcus Aurelius's *Meditations*
Friedrich Nietzsche's *On the Genealogy of Morality*
Friedrich Nietzsche's *Beyond Good and Evil*
Plato's *Republic*
Plato's *Symposium*
Jean-Jacques Rousseau's *The Social Contract*
Gilbert Ryle's *The Concept of Mind*
Baruch Spinoza's *Ethics*
Sun Tzu's *The Art of War*
Ludwig Wittgenstein's *Philosophical Investigations*

POLITICS

Benedict Anderson's *Imagined Communities*
Aristotle's *Politics*
Bernard Bailyn's *The Ideological Origins of the American Revolution*
Edmund Burke's *Reflections on the Revolution in France*
John C. Calhoun's *A Disquisition on Government*
Ha-Joon Chang's *Kicking Away the Ladder*
Hamid Dabashi's *Iran: A People Interrupted*
Hamid Dabashi's *Theology of Discontent: The Ideological Foundation of the Islamic Revolution in Iran*
Robert Dahl's *Democracy and its Critics*
Robert Dahl's *Who Governs?*
David Brion Davis's *The Problem of Slavery in the Age of Revolution*

Alexis De Tocqueville's *Democracy in America*
James Ferguson's *The Anti-Politics Machine*
Frank Dikotter's *Mao's Great Famine*
Sheila Fitzpatrick's *Everyday Stalinism*
Eric Foner's *Reconstruction: America's Unfinished Revolution, 1863-1877*
Milton Friedman's *Capitalism and Freedom*
Francis Fukuyama's *The End of History and the Last Man*
John Lewis Gaddis's *We Now Know: Rethinking Cold War History*
Ernest Gellner's *Nations and Nationalism*
David Graeber's *Debt: the First 5000 Years*
Antonio Gramsci's *The Prison Notebooks*
Alexander Hamilton, John Jay & James Madison's *The Federalist Papers*
Friedrich Hayek's *The Road to Serfdom*
Christopher Hill's *The World Turned Upside Down*
Thomas Hobbes's *Leviathan*
John A. Hobson's *Imperialism: A Study*
Samuel P. Huntington's *The Clash of Civilizations and the Remaking of World Order*
Tony Judt's *Postwar: A History of Europe Since 1945*
David C. Kang's *China Rising: Peace, Power and Order in East Asia*
Paul Kennedy's *The Rise and Fall of Great Powers*
Robert Keohane's *After Hegemony*
Martin Luther King Jr.'s *Why We Can't Wait*
Henry Kissinger's *World Order: Reflections on the Character of Nations and the Course of History*
John Locke's *Two Treatises of Government*
Niccolò Machiavelli's *The Prince*
Thomas Robert Malthus's *An Essay on the Principle of Population*
Mahmood Mamdani's *Citizen and Subject: Contemporary Africa And The Legacy Of Late Colonialism*
Karl Marx's *Capital*
John Stuart Mill's *On Liberty*
John Stuart Mill's *Utilitarianism*
Hans Morgenthau's *Politics Among Nations*
Thomas Paine's *Common Sense*
Thomas Paine's *Rights of Man*
Thomas Piketty's *Capital in the Twenty-First Century*
Robert D. Putman's *Bowling Alone*
John Rawls's *Theory of Justice*
Jean-Jacques Rousseau's *The Social Contract*
Theda Skocpol's *States and Social Revolutions*
Adam Smith's *The Wealth of Nations*
Sun Tzu's *The Art of War*
Henry David Thoreau's *Civil Disobedience*
Thucydides's *The History of the Peloponnesian War*
Kenneth Waltz's *Theory of International Politics*
Max Weber's *Politics as a Vocation*
Odd Arne Westad's *The Global Cold War: Third World Interventions And The Making Of Our Times*

POSTCOLONIAL STUDIES

Roland Barthes's *Mythologies*
Frantz Fanon's *Black Skin, White Masks*
Homi K. Bhabha's *The Location of Culture*
Gustavo Gutiérrez's *A Theology of Liberation*
Edward Said's *Orientalism*
Gayatri Chakravorty Spivak's *Can the Subaltern Speak?*

PSYCHOLOGY

Gordon Allport's *The Nature of Prejudice*
Alan Baddeley & Graham Hitch's *Aggression: A Social Learning Analysis*
Albert Bandura's *Aggression: A Social Learning Analysis*
Leon Festinger's *A Theory of Cognitive Dissonance*
Sigmund Freud's *The Interpretation of Dreams*
Betty Friedan's *The Feminine Mystique*
Michael R. Gottfredson & Travis Hirschi's *A General Theory of Crime*
Eric Hoffer's *The True Believer: Thoughts on the Nature of Mass Movements*
William James's *Principles of Psychology*
Elizabeth Loftus's *Eyewitness Testimony*
A. H. Maslow's *A Theory of Human Motivation*
Stanley Milgram's *Obedience to Authority*
Steven Pinker's *The Better Angels of Our Nature*
Oliver Sacks's *The Man Who Mistook His Wife For a Hat*
Richard Thaler & Cass Sunstein's *Nudge: Improving Decisions About Health, Wealth and Happiness*
Amos Tversky's *Judgment under Uncertainty: Heuristics and Biases*
Philip Zimbardo's *The Lucifer Effect*

SCIENCE

Rachel Carson's *Silent Spring*
William Cronon's *Nature's Metropolis: Chicago And The Great West*
Alfred W. Crosby's *The Columbian Exchange*
Charles Darwin's *On the Origin of Species*
Richard Dawkin's *The Selfish Gene*
Thomas Kuhn's *The Structure of Scientific Revolutions*
Geoffrey Parker's *Global Crisis: War, Climate Change and Catastrophe in the Seventeenth Century*
Mathis Wackernagel & William Rees's *Our Ecological Footprint*

SOCIOLOGY

Michelle Alexander's *The New Jim Crow: Mass Incarceration in the Age of Colorblindness*
Gordon Allport's *The Nature of Prejudice*
Albert Bandura's *Aggression: A Social Learning Analysis*
Hanna Batatu's *The Old Social Classes And The Revolutionary Movements Of Iraq*
Ha-Joon Chang's *Kicking Away the Ladder*
W. E. B. Du Bois's *The Souls of Black Folk*
Émile Durkheim's *On Suicide*
Frantz Fanon's *Black Skin, White Masks*
Frantz Fanon's *The Wretched of the Earth*
Eric Foner's *Reconstruction: America's Unfinished Revolution, 1863-1877*
Eugene Genovese's *Roll, Jordan, Roll: The World the Slaves Made*
Jack Goldstone's *Revolution and Rebellion in the Early Modern World*
Antonio Gramsci's *The Prison Notebooks*
Richard Herrnstein & Charles A Murray's *The Bell Curve: Intelligence and Class Structure in American Life*
Eric Hoffer's *The True Believer: Thoughts on the Nature of Mass Movements*
Jane Jacobs's *The Death and Life of Great American Cities*
Robert Lucas's *Why Doesn't Capital Flow from Rich to Poor Countries?*
Jay Macleod's *Ain't No Makin' It: Aspirations and Attainment in a Low Income Neighborhood*
Elaine May's *Homeward Bound: American Families in the Cold War Era*
Douglas McGregor's *The Human Side of Enterprise*
C. Wright Mills's *The Sociological Imagination*

Thomas Piketty's *Capital in the Twenty-First Century*
Robert D. Putman's *Bowling Alone*
David Riesman's *The Lonely Crowd: A Study of the Changing American Character*
Edward Said's *Orientalism*
Joan Wallach Scott's *Gender and the Politics of History*
Theda Skocpol's *States and Social Revolutions*
Max Weber's *The Protestant Ethic and the Spirit of Capitalism*

THEOLOGY

Augustine's *Confessions*
Benedict's *Rule of St Benedict*
Gustavo Gutiérrez's *A Theology of Liberation*
Carole Hillenbrand's *The Crusades: Islamic Perspectives*
David Hume's *Dialogues Concerning Natural Religion*
Immanuel Kant's *Religion within the Boundaries of Mere Reason*
Ernst Kantorowicz's *The King's Two Bodies: A Study in Medieval Political Theology*
Søren Kierkegaard's *The Sickness Unto Death*
C. S. Lewis's *The Abolition of Man*
Saba Mahmood's *The Politics of Piety: The Islamic Revival and the Feminist Subject*
Baruch Spinoza's *Ethics*
Keith Thomas's *Religion and the Decline of Magic*

COMING SOON

Chris Argyris's *The Individual and the Organisation*
Seyla Benhabib's *The Rights of Others*
Walter Benjamin's *The Work Of Art in the Age of Mechanical Reproduction*
John Berger's *Ways of Seeing*
Pierre Bourdieu's *Outline of a Theory of Practice*
Mary Douglas's *Purity and Danger*
Roland Dworkin's *Taking Rights Seriously*
James G. March's *Exploration and Exploitation in Organisational Learning*
Ikujiro Nonaka's *A Dynamic Theory of Organizational Knowledge Creation*
Griselda Pollock's *Vision and Difference*
Amartya Sen's *Inequality Re-Examined*
Susan Sontag's *On Photography*
Yasser Tabbaa's *The Transformation of Islamic Art*
Ludwig von Mises's *Theory of Money and Credit*

The Macat Library By Discipline